100

THINGS TO DO IN
FORT MYERS & SANIBEL
BEFORE YOU
DIE

100

THINGS TO DO IN
FORT MYERS & SANIBEL
BEFORE YOU
DIE

. . . .

NANCY HAMILTON

REEDY PRESS

Library of Congress Control Number: 2017957318

ISBN: 9781681061276

Design by Jill Halpin

Cover photo: Courtesy of Ilene Safron

Printed in the United States of America
18 19 20 21 22   5 4 3 2

Please note that websites, phone numbers, addresses, and company names are subject to change or cancellation. We did our best to relay the most accurate information available, but due to circumstances beyond our control, please do not hold us liable for misinformation. When exploring new destinations, please do your homework before you go.

DEDICATION

To Eddie, Madalyn, and the friends
who are taking the journey with me.

CONTENTS

• •

Music and Entertainment

• •

Sports and Recreation

● ●

Culture and History

• •

Shopping and Fashion

• •

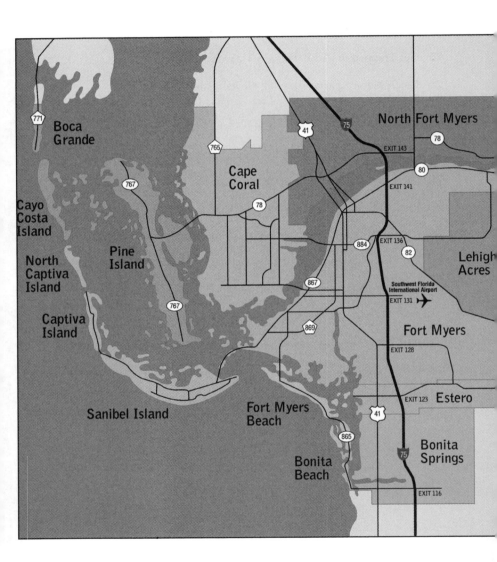

PREFACE

Whether you are driving Interstate 75 or flying into Southwest Florida International Airport (RSW) to arrive in Fort Myers, you are about to discover one of the top locations in North America to relax and reconnect with family and friends. The vibrant and artsy city of Fort Myers paired with the pristine white sand beaches strewn with seashells bordering the warm Gulf of Mexico waters of Sanibel and the neighboring islands allow you to disconnect from pressures and begin your explorations of the *100 Things to Do in Fort Myers & Sanibel Before You Die.*

First discovered by the native Calusas, then Spanish explorers, the city once prompted winter resident Thomas Edison to say, "There is only one Fort Myers in the United States, and there are ninety million people who are going to find it out." Visitors come by boat to explore the subtropical islands, by car to tour historic and cultural sites, and by bike and on foot to witness up close the abundant wildlife.

Offering a host of discoverable treasures, the area covered by this book includes: Sanibel and Captiva Islands, Fort Myers Beach, Fort Myers, Bonita Springs–Estero, Cape Coral, Pine Island & Matlacha, Boca Grande, and more than one hundred coastal islands off the mainland, along with North Fort Myers and inland communities. Collectively, the region affords a near-endless spectrum of recreational and educational opportunities.

• •

FUN FACTS

The first tourist to reach Southwest Florida was Spanish explorer Ponce de Leon, who visited Pine Island in 1513 and was later mortally wounded in these same waters by a Calusa Indian arrow.

Fort Myers's McGregor Boulevard is lined on both sides with statuesque royal palm trees; Thomas Edison had the first group of palms imported from Cuba and planted along this main thoroughfare.

The sport of tarpon fishing originated in Southwest Florida's Pine Island Sound in the late 1880s, and Boca Grande Pass, the waterway between Cayo Costa and Gasparilla Island, is considered the "Tarpon Fishing Capital of the World."

Thomas Edison, who spent many winters in Fort Myers, is considered the most inventive man who ever lived, holding 1,093 patents for everything from lightbulbs, cement, and phonographs to the natural rubber he made from goldenrod. He was named *Life* magazine's Man of the Millennium.

Area beaches are ranked some of the best in the world for shelling, with more varieties found here than anywhere else in North America. The shelling position is so common that it's given a name—the Sanibel Stoop.

You can boat straight across the state of Florida from Fort Myers/Sanibel to Palm Beach via the Caloosahatchee River and Okeechobee Waterway; both are part of the Intracoastal Waterway.

• •

The banyan tree at the Edison Winter Home is one of the largest specimens in the United States. The tree's aerial roots now have a circumference of more than four hundred feet.

Koreshan State Park in Estero commemorates an eccentric religious sect that believed the world to be a hollow globe, with mankind residing on the inner surface gazing into the universe below.

Anne Morrow Lindbergh, the wife of America's famous aviator, wrote her best-selling book *Gift from the Sea* without ever identifying her inspiration as Captiva Island.

Some of the original European settlers to the area were flower growers from the Benelux region of the continent. At one time their horticultural efforts made Fort Myers the "Gladiolus Capital of the World."

Calusa Indian culture, carbon dated to 1150 BC, had its cultural center in Southwest Florida. Although the tribe is now extinct, ceremonial, burial, and refuse shell mounds are found on Mound Key, Pine Island, Cabbage Key, Useppa Island, and elsewhere in the vicinity.

• •

ACKNOWLEDGMENTS

Sincere thanks to the many people who have provided the details for *100 Things,* including those who work, play, and enjoy the extraordinary place we call home. Special thanks goes to staff at the Visitor & Convention Bureau and other Lee County employees who helped confirm obscure facts. My deepest gratitude goes to Chelle Koster Walton for making the book better. Also, cheers to Ilene Safron, Mike Shapiro, and Kelly Stephens for their contributions. Finally, my heartfelt thanks are sent out to my travel friends who encouraged me every step of the way.

Photo Credit:
Courtesy of Ilene Safron

FOOD AND DRINK

PEEL AND EAT
PINK GOLD SHRIMP

In the heyday of the '50s and '60s, Fort Myers Beach had one of the largest shrimp ports in the United States. It was the discovery of pink shrimp, considered the gold standard, that led the way. At night, the "cowboys of the sea" would head out on the Gulf of Mexico to net these delicacies, considered sweeter and cleaner than other local species. Today, most of the pink gold is sent to restaurants in the Northeast, but you can sample it locally at Bonita Bill's Waterfront Cafe, a casual dock restaurant under the Matanzas Pass Bridge. Once you try the shrimp, you can learn more about this delicacy and the local seafood industry by joining a three-hour waterfront tour with the Ostego Bay Marine Science Center.

Bonita Bill's Waterfront Cafe
702 Fisherman's Wharf,
Fort Myers Beach 33931
239-463-6119
bonitabills.com

Ostego Bay Marine Science Center
718 Fisherman's Wharf,
Fort Myers Beach 33931
239-765-8101
ostegobay.org

TIP
To get your fill of shrimp, attend the annual Fort Myers Beach Shrimp Festival & Parade held in late February or early March. The festival date is chosen by the full moon because no shrimping is done when the light casts a shadow from their nets, so the fleet is in port for the festival. Visit fortmyersbeachshrimpfestival.com for more information.

SAMPLE THE OCEAN
FOR SUCCULENT SEAFOOD

When staying along the Gulf of Mexico, you have many options when it comes to ocean cuisine. While almost all local restaurants serve fresh seafood and fish, here are a few top choices for sampling the treasures of the ocean while enjoying different settings. First is the Blue Dog Bar & Grill, an American gastropub, set in an old fishing village-turned-artist colony, that serves up plenty of shrimp and other popular dishes. Other choices include Fresh Catch Bistro, where you can catch a spectacular Gulf beach sunset while sampling its cranberry and candied pecan-encrusted grouper. At Gramma Dot's you can watch the boats at the Sanibel Marina while tasting grouper served in a salad, sandwich, or entrée. While your curry red snapper is cooking at Captiva House, you can view original drawings of editorial cartoonist and conservationist J. N. "Ding" Darling, who had his studio at 'Tween Waters Inn.

Blue Dog Bar & Grill
Matlacha Pass Aquatic Preserve
4597 Pine Island Rd., Matlacha 33993
239-558-4970
bluedogrestaurant.com

Fresh Catch Bistro Lounge and Raw Bar
3040 Estero Blvd., Fort Myers Beach 33931
239-463-2600
freshcatchbistro.com

Gramma Dot's Seaside Saloon
634 N. Yachtsman Dr., Sanibel 33957
239-472-8138
sanibelmarina.com

Captiva House
'Tween Waters Inn, 15951 Captiva Dr., Captiva 33924
239-472-5161
captiva-house.com

Tarpon Bay Restaurant
Hyatt Regency Coconut Point Resort and Spa
5001 Coconut Rd., Bonita Springs 34134
239-390-4295
coconutpoint.regency.hyatt.com

Bayfront Bistro
4761 Estero Blvd., Fort Myers Beach 33931
239-463-3663
bayfrontbistro.com

Blue Pointe Oyster Bar & Seafood Grill
13499 S. Cleveland Ave., Fort Myers 33907
239-433-0634
bluepointerestaurant.com

Courtney's Continental Cuisine
20351 Summerlin Rd., #111, Fort Myers 33908
239-466-4646
courtneyscontinentalcuisine.com

Flipper's on the Bay
Lovers Key Resort
8771 Estero Blvd., Fort Myers Beach 33931
239-765-1025
flippersotb.com

Keylime Bistro at Captiva Island Inn
11509 Andy Rosse Ln., Captiva 33924
239-395-4000
keylimebistrocaptiva.com

The Prawnbroker Restaurant & Fish Market
13451-16 McGregor Blvd., Fort Myers 33919
239-489-2226
prawnbrokerfortmyers.com

The Timbers Restaurant & Fish Market
703 Tarpon Bay Rd., Sanibel 33957
239-395-CRAB (2722)
timbersofsanibel.com

University Grill
7790 Cypress Lake Dr., Fort Myers 33907
239-437-4377
universitygrill.net

WAKE UP—
YOU'LL BE GLAD YOU DID

Morning risers will be happy they got up early when the smells from the Heavenly Biscuit waft their way. Tucked away in a colorful cottage on Fort Myers Beach, the restaurant offers an affordable limited menu for breakfast and lunch. The cinnamon rolls and biscuits are, well, heavenly. If you're more in the mood for a full-range breakfast served all day, you can instead head to Sanibel's Lighthouse Cafe. While dining on the Seafood Benedict or the Hungry Fishermen omelet, you can take a gander at the hundreds of lighthouse photographs on the walls. Call-ahead seating is available for this popular restaurant. Heading out with the kids? No problem. Families will find great choices in the cow-themed and colorfully decorated Reese's Restaurant, famous for its Mickey Mouse pancakes, or The Island Cow, known for its "eggs-tensive" menu items and its TVs showing cartoons.

Heavenly Biscuit
110 Mango St.,
Fort Myers Beach 33931
239-463-7600

Lighthouse Cafe
362 Periwinkle Way, Sanibel 33957
239-472-0303
lighthousecafe.com

Reese's Restaurant
1661 Estero Blvd., Ste. 7,
Fort Myers Beach 33931
239-463-3933

The Island Cow
2163 Periwinkle Way,
Sanibel 33957
239-472-0606
sanibelislandcow.com

SEEK COMFORT FOOD AND FRIENDLY SERVICE
AT THE OASIS

Those seeking a warm, friendly smile while visiting a new city should stop in at The Oasis Restaurant in downtown Fort Myers. It is the "Cheers" of Fort Myers. Not only does everyone get to know your name, but guests might also get a hug from the owners, Bonnie Grunberg and Tammie Shockey. Their specials are fabulous and filling. Favorites include chicken Parmesan, homemade soups, and salads and wraps. When diners don't see something they're yearning for on the menu, they can just ask for it. If the kitchen has the ingredients, the food will be whipped up especially for you. Try to make a reservation for this popular spot, particularly at lunchtime, when downtown workers head in.

2260 Dr. Martin Luther King Jr. Blvd., Fort Myers 33901
239-334-1566
oasisatfortmyers.com

TIP
Be sure to ask for a "to-go cup" to continue quenching your thirst, very important in a Southern climate.

FIGHT
WORLD HUNGER

A Christian ministry formed Educational Concerns for Hunger Organization (ECHO) to fight world hunger. Located in North Fort Myers, this nonprofit organization invites visitors to tour its experimental farm and discover how agricultural solutions are being used by those working with the poor in more than 180 countries. The two-hour tour allows you to see and taste a variety of rare and nutritious foods from an exotic collection of tropical fruit trees and edible plants—the largest collection of its kind in the continental United States. If you're interested in growing some plants of your own, be sure to watch the Urban Garden demonstration to learn how to grow plants without using soil. Many of the seeds and plants are available for purchase in the Global Nursery and bookstore.

ECHO Global Farm
17391 Durrance Rd., North Fort Myers 33917
239-543-3246
echonet.org

TIP
Agritourists can check online at ifas.ufl.edu for the date of the annual Lee County Urban Farm Tour, sponsored by the University of Florida IFAS extension.

EAT CLEAN
AT LOCAL FARMS

What fresher way to dine than to pull up a chair at the farmer's table? Buckingham Farms is a hydroponic farm that won the 2015 Chrysalis Award in Sustainability, as recognized by the local business community. Enjoy farmhouse favorites for breakfast and lunch onsite at The Rustic Barn or try the Friday dinner-to-go menu before hitting up the country store. From Julio's hash to the crab cake BLT, all dishes are made with natural ingredients. As an alternative, head to Rosy Tomorrows Heritage Farm, which just won the 2017 Chrysalis Eco-Innovation Award. A sustainable farm that uses organic and holistic practices, Rosy's features 100 percent grass-fed Longhorn cows and pastured animals such as pigs and chickens. On Saturday Market Days, visitors are invited to see animals, feed alfalfa to the cows and miniature donkeys, and enjoy a delicious brunch based on the bounty of the one-hundred-acre farm.

Buckingham Farms
12931 Orange River Blvd., Fort Myers 33905
239-206-2303
buckinghamfarmsonline.com

Rosy Tomorrows Heritage Farm
8250 Nalle Grade Rd., North Fort Myers 33917
239-567-6000
rosy-tomorrows.com

FIND SOUTHERN COMFORT
AT THE FARMERS MARKET RESTAURANT

If it's Southern comfort you seek, the Farmers Market Restaurant has it waiting for you. Opened in 1952 in a small building in front of the State Farmers Market, it is the longest-operating restaurant in Lee County. Original owner Bill Barnwell served farmers and truck drivers moving the produce to market. Now an institution, the restaurant is owned and operated by Barnwell's son and daughter-in-law, Chip and Betsy. It offers a variety of Southern- and country-fried foods, including chicken; non-fried options such as meatloaf; and for healthier options: a two-, four-, or five-vegetable plate. This is where you'll find fried green tomatoes, fresh collard greens, and stewed okra. Food is prepared from scratch. Are you hungry yet?

2736 Edison Ave., Fort Myers 33916
239-334-1687
farmersmarketrestaurant.com

FEAST YOUR EYES AND YOUR PALATE
ON THIS LOCAL FAVORITE

Come hungry when you arrive at the Bubble Room Restaurant, founded in 1979 on Captiva Island. The colorful and whimsical exterior gives you a glimpse of what's to come. The minute you walk through the door, the nostalgic décor and the dessert cases are a feast for the eyes. Originally, the decorations—'30s and '40s memorabilia—were concentrated in one room of the former home. Over the past decades, however, both the restaurant and the collection have expanded to feature three floors of Old Florida, Hollywood, and Christmas collectibles. Prevalent throughout, of course, are the bubble lights. Start with Bubble Bread, followed by Smoke Gets in Your Eyes, The Great Gatsby, or the Duck Ellington—you get the idea. But the most difficult choice is dessert. Red velvet and orange crunch cakes are scrumptious favorites.

15001 Captiva Dr., Captiva 33924
239-472-5558
bubbleroomrestaurant.com

TIP
For a meal that is lighter on your stomach (and wallet), try the Tiny Bubble. Also, it is suggested that you arrive at opening time, as the restaurant is extremely popular and doesn't take reservations.

SAVOR SOPHISTICATED SEAFOOD
AT SUNSET

From longtime favorite to new kid on the block, fine dining can be found in the islands' restaurant scene. For one, there is The Mad Hatter, which has been a staple on the islands for more than thirty years. Based in a beach bungalow on the Gulf, it is only open for romantic dinners. Savor black truffle sea scallops while the sun is setting. Another prime choice is the Tarpon Lodge Restaurant, where you can try blue crab while enjoying the sunset on Pine Island Sound. Or why not go to Sweet Melissa's Cafe, with its sophisticated décor and imaginative food combinations? Try BBQ shrimp and grits, a recipe that goes back to Chef Melissa Talmage's roots working at Commander's Palace in New Orleans.

The Mad Hatter
6467 Sanibel-Captiva Rd.,
Sanibel 33957
239-472-0033
madhatterrestaurant.com

Tarpon Lodge Restaurant
13771 Waterfront Dr.,
Bokeelia 33922
239-283-3999
tarponlodge.com

Sweet Melissa's Cafe, 1625 Periwinkle Way, Sanibel 33957
239-472-1956 sweetmelissascafe.com

TIP
These are extremely popular restaurants; reservations are recommended.

GET DRESSED UP
TO SAMPLE SOUTHERN CHARM

Put on your heels and dinner jacket—the award-winning Veranda offers Southern cuisine and hospitality in the downtown Fort Myers Historic District. Opened in 1978, it is housed in two side-by-side early-twentieth-century homes that have become the setting for special-occasion celebrations. Whether guests are dining in the outdoor garden or in the living room near the fireplace, the ambience can only be beat by the delicious food. Start with the honey wheat with oatmeal molasses bread, followed by fried green tomatoes, and then perhaps the scrumptious Southern Sampler of seafood. Save room for the housemade desserts. All this can be accompanied by a choice from the extensive wine list featuring by-the-glass selections served from a Cruvinet. For a new place to find Southern delights, try Cork Soakers Deck & Wine Bar in Cape Coral.

The Veranda
2122 Second St. at Broadway,
Fort Myers 33901
239-332-2065
verandarestaurant.com

Cork Soakers Deck & Wine Bar
837 SE 47th Ter., Cape Coral 33904
239-542-6622
corksoakers.net

TIP
Reservations are accepted and can be easily made on The Veranda's website through OpenTable.

DROP IN FOR A LATTE,
A POUND OF SHRIMP, OR A HAMMER

The second-oldest business in Lee County, Bailey's General Store, was started in 1899 by Frank Bailey as the Sanibel Packing Company to pack and ship produce. As Sanibel Island's economy shifted from agriculture to tourism, the needs of islanders changed, as did the store. The full-service, customer-friendly market is part traditional grocery, part hardware store. It stocks produce, seafood, and a butcher's shop, along with tools, gifts, and beachwear. Now, third- and fourth-generation Baileys are at the helm, implementing new additions such as the Coffee Bar, where locals and visitors alike meet to chat over a morning cup of fresh brew. In 2016 the store earned the LocalLEE Grown Business Award, which is presented for a business's contributions to the local economy through growth and innovation, industry leadership, or display of superior corporate citizenship. Bailey's does it all.

2477 Periwinkle Way, Sanibel 33957
239-472-1516
baileys-sanibel.com

TIP
Visitors can go online and order a Vacation Starter Package consisting of typical grocery items needed for their stay on the island. Bailey's will deliver the order, or visitors can pick it up curbside.

SET THE BAR SKY HIGH:
TAKING IT ROOFTOP

What better place to relax under the stars with waterfront views and live tunes than a sky bar? In the downtown Fort Myers Historic District, you can walk between your choices. First stop: the eighth floor of Hotel Indigo and its Rooftop Bar & Lounge. Enjoy your favorite beverage while feasting your eyes on stunning views of the Caloosahatchee River. Next stop: The Firestone Skybar, where cocktails come with an eyeful of the Downtown River Basin and Centennial Park. For a rooftop view of the Gulf of Mexico, head to Fort Myers Beach and The Beached Whale's Lookout Lounge in the Times Square area. Typically Fort Myers Beach, this place rocks your flip-flops off.

Hotel Indigo Fort Myers
1520 Broadway, #104, Fort Myers 33901
239-337-3446
hotelftmyers.com

The Firestone Skybar
2224 Bay St., Fort Myers 33901
239-334-FIRE (3473)
firestonefl.com

The Beached Whale Lookout Lounge
1249 Estero Blvd., Fort Myers Beach 33931
239-463-5505
thebeachedwhale.com

ESCAPE LIFE
BY VISITING AN ISLAND

Water permeates Southwest Florida—from the Gulf of Mexico and the Caloosahatchee River to any number of bays and estuaries. Add in the region's mild year-round weather and you have the perfect formula for a boatload of by-boat dining destinations. For unbridged destinations such as Cabbage Key Inn and Restaurant, boating is the only way to arrive at the eponymous one-hundred-acre subtropical island. Boaters stop to score a "Cheeseburger in Paradise" along with seafood brought in fresh by local fishermen. Guests can dine daily in the green room, where diners have taped autographed dollar bills many layers thick to the walls of the historic mid-1930s house. Check out the framed dollars behind the bar signed by patrons such as Jimmy Buffett, Julia Roberts, and John F. Kennedy Jr. Or choose a seat under the palm trees atop the inn's hilltop perch overlooking the marina.

P.O. Box 200, Pineland 33945
Channel Marker 60
239-283-2278
cabbagekey.com

TIP
Check in at one of the rustic rooms in the inn or rent a cottage for an extended getaway. A climb up the water tower allows a 360-degree view of the island.

By boat or car

Coconut Jack's
5370 Bonita Beach, Bonita Springs 34134
239-676-7777
coconutjacks.com

Doc Ford's Rum Bar & Grille
708 Fisherman's Wharf, Fort Myers Beach 33931
239-765-9660
docfords.com

Flipper's on the Bay at Lovers Key Resort
Lovers Key Resort
8771 Estero Blvd., Fort Myers Beach 33931
239-765-1025
flippersotb.com

Nervous Nellie's
1131 First St., Fort Myers Beach 33931
239-463-8077
nervousnellies.net

Pinchers Crab Shack
The Marina at Edison Ford, 2360 West 1st St.,
Fort Myers 33901
239-245-7049
pinchersusa.com

Parrot Key Caribbean Grill
Salty Sam's Marina, 2500 Main St.,
Fort Myers Beach 33931
239-463-3257
myparrotkey.com

Rumrunners
5848 Cape Harbour Dr., Cape Coral 33914
239-542-0200
rumrunnersrestaurant.com

FEEL NOSTALGIC
WHILE DINING

Some of the downtown area's themed restaurants feed on the notions of good American food and the neighborhood's rich history of famous winter residents. The trend started in 2008 with Daniel Kearns's opening of The Edison for dining and nightlife. Located one mile south of the world-famous Edison & Ford Winter Estates, the restaurant pays tribute to one of Fort Myers's favorite past residents, inventor Thomas Edison. In 2012 came Ford's Garage, in honor of Edison's next-door neighbor, Henry Ford. In the setting of a '20s service station/Prohibition bar, Ford's Garage showcases a Model A Ford, old-fashioned fuel pumps, and gas pump nozzles for front-door handles. Other "neighbors" include The Firestone Grill Room, named for "tire king" Harvey Firestone, and Capone's Coal Fired Pizza, recreating the jazz age of gangster Al Capone.

TIP
Be sure to check out each restaurant's restrooms, which creatively embellish the nostalgic themes.

Edison Restaurant, Bar and Banquet Center
3583 McGregor Blvd., Fort Myers 33901
239-936-9348
edisonfl.com

Ford's Garage
2207 First St., Fort Myers 33901
239-332-FORD (3673)
fordsgarageusa.com

The Firestone Grill Room • Martini Bar • Skybar
2224 Bay St., Fort Myers 33901
239-334-FIRE (3473)
firestonefl.com

Capone's Coal Fired Pizza
2225 First St., Fort Myers 33901
239-337-COAL (2625)
caponescoalfiredpizza.com

EATING AT LOCAL CHAINS
PROVIDES A TASTE OF THE DESTINATION

While many people like to eat at chain restaurants because they know what kind of food to expect, it is local flavor that gives visitors a true taste of the destination. Pinchers Crab Shack, a family-owned operation, serves up seafood from local fishermen and crabbers. Also served up by a local fisherman and author, Doc Ford's Rum Bar & Grille was named for the protagonist in a series of murder mystery novels. Fishing captain Randy Wayne White used to sell his catch at the same location as the first Doc Ford's restaurant before becoming a *New York Times* best-selling author. Now the rum bar is known for its fish tacos, Yucatan shrimp, and other seafood delights.

Pinchers Crab Shack
The Marina at Edison Ford,
2360 W. First St., Fort Myers 33901
239-245-7049
pinchersusa.com

Doc Ford's Rum Bar & Grille
2500 Island Inn Rd., Sanibel 33957
239-472-8311
docfords.com

TIP

At the restaurant, pick up one of the Doc Ford books for a great beach read. Start with *Sanibel Flats,* placed on the 100 Favorite Mysteries of the 20th Century by the Independent Mystery Booksellers Association.

COOL OFF
AT A LOCAL HOT SPOT

When it's hot in Florida you reach for a cold one, especially after a tough round on the course . . . miniature golf with the family can be so grueling! Local sweet spots for homemade ice cream, yogurt, sorbet, and gelato can provide the respite you need. Head out to enjoy a scoop at these salons, diners, parlors, and take-out windows.

Artisan Gelato by Norman Love
11300 Lindbergh Blvd., #112,
Fort Myers 33913
239-288-4333
normanloveconfections.com/
artisan-gelato

Love Boat Premium
Homemade Ice Cream
16475 San Carlos Blvd.,
Fort Myers 33908
239-466-7707
loveboaticecream.com

Daddy Dee's Ice Cream Parlor
13161 N. Cleveland Ave., #1,
North Fort Myers 33903
239-997-4021
facebook.com/daddydeesicecream

Queenie's Homemade Ice Cream
16681 McGregor Blvd., #308,
Fort Myers 33908
239-432-0098
queeniesicecream.com

Royal Scoop Homemade Ice Cream
15 8th St., Bonita Springs 34134
239-992-2000
royalscoop.com

TIP
Royal Scoop hosts many free community events throughout the year, including its extremely popular annual Easter egg hunt. Check the calendar on its website when you are in town.

LIFT YOUR SPIRITS
AND YOUR GLASS

To lift your spirits, try some local grog at the family-run Wicked Dolphin Rum Distillery. It uses 100 percent Florida sugarcane and local ingredients aged in bourbon barrels to handcraft its small batches of award-winning rum. The distillery has even placed barrels to age at the bottom of the Gulf of Mexico aboard the USS *Mohawk,* sunk to create an artificial reef thirty miles off Sanibel's coast. While Wicked Dolphin offers reserve and premium rums, it also has the offbeat strawberry, blueberry, and apple pie flavored rums. Take a free sixty-minute tour to learn the steps from cooking to distilling and what influences the rum's color and taste. Then, sample the goods in the tasting room. For a wide range of spirits plus a tour, try family-owned List Distillery. Using locally sourced crops and organic ingredients, it offers vodka, gin, rum, and white whiskey.

Wicked Dolphin Rum Distillery
131 SW 3rd Pl., Cape Coral 33991
239-242-5244
wickeddolphinrum.com

List Distillery
3680 Evans Ave., Fort Myers 33901
239-208-7214
listdistillery.com

DIG YOUR TOES IN THE SAND
TO TOAST GULF OF MEXICO SUNSETS

Dig your toes in the sand to toast sunset on the Gulf of Mexico at the Mucky Duck, the Outrigger Beach Resort Tiki Bar, and Doc's Beach House. At the Mucky Duck, locals, snowbirds, and visitors all perch on picnic tables to enjoy a cool one while the sun dips into the Gulf. The beat picks up as the Tiki Bar rocks with live music, a thirty-two-ounce Bucket of Fun libation, and conch blowing at sunset on Fort Myers Beach. Further south, Doc's Beach House is the perfect casual place to stop along Bonita Beach for a sip of wine or beer with a Chicago-style pizza at sunset.

Mucky Duck
11546 Andy Rosse Ln.,
Captiva 33924
239-472-3434, muckyduck.com

Outrigger Beach Resort Tiki Bar
6200 Estero Blvd.,
Fort Myers Beach 33931
239-463-3131, outriggerfmb.com

Doc's Beach House
27908 Hickory Blvd., Bonita Springs 34134
239-992-6444, docsbeachhouse.com

TIP
As the sun dips almost entirely into the Gulf, be sure to watch for the green flash, an optical phenomenon that reveals itself when the ocean is flat, the sky is clear, and the middle spectrum of light shows green for a split second or two. It is the aurora borealis of Florida.

TAKE IN A FLIGHT
AS LOCAL BREWERIES TAKE OFF

What better to do on a hot day than sample a flight at one of the local craft breweries? The Fort Myers Brewing Company is a local favorite with thirty-plus inhouse brews to choose from as well as special events like Trivia Night Tuesday or Food Truck Thursday. Be sure to bring a chair, as there is an overflow out the door. Point Ybel Brewing Company is a small-batch brewery that features beach-themed beers. Trivia Night is Wednesday, while Jazz Night—highlighting local musicians—is Thursday. Big Blue Brewing uses locally sourced products including fresh Florida juices, honey, produce, and steaks from cattle raised by the Seminole tribe. In return, Big Blue gives the leftover grain from the brewing process to the tribe to feed the cattle.

Fort Myers Brewing Company
12811 Commerce Lakes Dr.,
Ste. 28, Fort Myers 33913
239-313-6576
fmbrew.com

Point Ybel Brewing Company
16120 San Carlos Blvd., #4,
Fort Myers 33908
239-603-6535
pointybelbrew.com

Big Blue Brewing
4721 SE 10th Pl., Cape Coral 33904
239-471-2777
bigbluebrewing.com

TIP
Many of the breweries offer tours. Call to check the schedule.

Bury Me Brewing
4224 S. Cleveland Ave., Fort Myers 33901
239-332-BEER (2337)
burymebrewing.com

Palm City Brewing
7887 Drew Cir., #130, Fort Myers 33967
239-362-2862
facebook.com/palmcitybrewing

Big Storm Brewing Company
839 Miramar St., Cape Coral 33904
239-257-1033
capecoralbrewing.com

Millennial Brewing Company
1811 Royal Palm Ave., Fort Myers 33901
239-271-2255
millennialbrewing.com

Momentum Brewhouse
9786 Bonita Beach Rd. SE, #1, Bonita Springs 34135
239-949-9945
momentumbrewhouse.com

Old Soul Brewing
10970 S. Cleveland Ave., #402, Fort Myers 33901
239-334-4334
oldsoulbrewing.com

FALL IN LOVE
WITH CHOCOLATY GOODNESS

Sweetness arrived in Fort Myers in 2001 when Norman Love Confections (NLC) opened, bringing gourmet chocolate to new heights. From barks to bonbons to bars of deliciousness, Love's confections capture taste buds in bites of white, dark, and milk chocolate. He soon added pastries, desserts, and gelatos to his many award-winning collections. In fact, just one year after its founding, NLC was selected by *USA Today* as one of the top ten artisan chocolate companies in the country. Since that early recognition, Love has received accolades from such people and professional organizations as *Saveur, Consumer Reports, Oprah,* and the *Robb Report*. He is perhaps most recognized, however, by his guest judge appearances on the Food Network's *Challenge* series. Want to try some of his famed recipes? Stop by one of his salons to sample fan favorites, including peanut butter and jelly, Key lime shell, and strawberry cheesecake.

1380 Lindbergh Blvd., Fort Myers 33913
239-561-7215
normanloveconfections.com

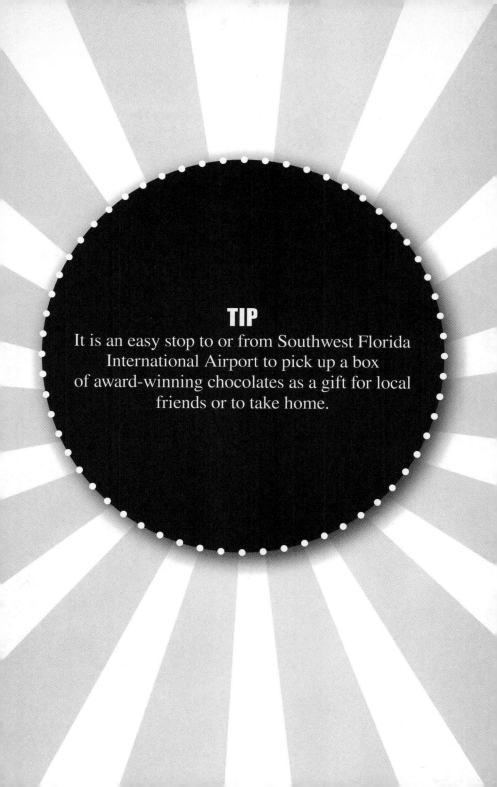

TIP

It is an easy stop to or from Southwest Florida
International Airport to pick up a box
of award-winning chocolates as a gift for local
friends or to take home.

MUSIC AND ENTERTAINMENT

COME FULLY TO YOUR SENSES
AT ARTFEST

Each February, downtown Fort Myers River District transforms into an open-air gallery that plays host to a three-day art extravaganza. ArtFest Fort Myers invites nine hundred artists from across the country to participate in a juried show, which pares down entries to the two hundred best exhibits. Art lovers can peruse the full realm of art media: jewelry, ceramics, wearable art, drawings, fiber, acrylic painting, watercolors, metal works, photography, sculpture, wood, graphics/printmaking, glass, digital, and combinations of media. The festival kicks off with an opening ticketed VIP Night, followed by two days of public exhibits to meet the artists; sample food, music, and art; and purchase some exquisite finds in a festive atmosphere. Children's activities include creating artwork—painting or sculpture—participating in the high school exhibit and competition, and watching teams in the chalk street painting contest.

1375 Monroe St., Fort Myers 33901
239-768-3602
artfestfortmyers.com

TIP
Check the website for details about reserving tickets for the VIP experience.

GROOVE TO THE
JAZZ BEAT

In 2007, Marc and Sherri Neeley brought a new jazz club to town. The Roadhouse Cafe is the sister restaurant to one on Cape Cod with the same name. Sherri's father, Brooklyn Dodger and famed trumpeter Lou Colombo, entertained patrons with his fabulous sound for many years. He once played with Dizzy Gillespie, Tony Bennett, Mel Tormé, and the Artie Shaw Orchestra before his untimely death in a 2012 auto accident. Colombo's family carries on the tradition of fine dining and live entertainment, featuring talented musicians and a Sunday night jazz jam. Find smooth music six nights a week, except summer months, when it's Wednesday through Sunday. If you're in Cape Coral, Slate's also entertains with jazz stylings. It serves up dinner and a Sunday jazz brunch with a New Orleans twist. Reservations are suggested at both restaurants.

Roadhouse Cafe
15660 San Carlos Blvd., # 280, Fort Myers 33908
239-415-4375
roadhousecafefl.com

Slate's
4820 Candia St., Cape Coral 33904
239-540-6800
slatescapecoral.com

PLAY A TUNE TO RECALL
A VACATION MEMORY

Music fans go wild over the tropical-tang tunes of vocal and visual artist Danny Morgan, whose songs just seem to fit their vacation memories like a broken-in flip-flop. "Oh Captiva, island of my dreams. You have stolen my heart . . ." His lyrics echo the sentiments of so many vacationers who hear him live at Casa Ybel Resort, Sundial Beach Resort & Spa, and Traders Gulf Coast Grill and Gifts on Sanibel. The musician has appeared on stage with The Beach Boys, Joe Cocker, Jimmy Buffett, and Pure Prairie League through the years. Morgan isn't the only one inspired to song by local settings, though. Crosby, Stills, Nash & Young recorded the song "Sanibel" on their album *Looking Forward,* while jazz great Michael Franks's "Barefoot on the Beach" is the title song of one of his popular CDs.

Casa Ybel Resort
2255 W. Gulf Dr., Sanibel 33957
239-472-3145
casaybelresort.com

Sundial Beach Resort & Spa
1451 Middle Gulf Dr.,
Sanibel 33957
239-472-4151
sundialresort.com

Traders Gulf Coast Grill and Gifts
1551 Periwinkle Way, Sanibel 33957
239-472-7242
traderssanibel.com

RIDE THE RAILS
FOR HISTORY AND MYSTERY

What better way to be entertained than by a murder mystery, especially when it's one served up with a five-course dinner on a retro train car? That's how the Murder Mystery Dinner Train rolls—a ride along the CSX rails for three-and-a-half hours while a comic mystery unfolds. Also for train buffs, the Railroad Museum of South Florida can be found within Lakes Regional Park. The museum houses artifacts, pictures, model railroads, and items from Florida railroads past. While there, ride the one-eighth-scale railroad as it travels through Lakes Park into areas only accessible by rail, passing miniature villages. And for a hidden gem, visit the free Gulf Coast Model Railroad at Shell Point Retirement Community. The forty-five-by-forty-one-foot running model train display re-creates the rails and trains of Florida.

Murder Mystery Dinner Train
2805 Colonial Blvd.,
Fort Myers 33966
239-275-8487
semgulf.com

Railroad Museum of South Florida
Lakes Regional Park,
7330 Gladiolus Dr.,
Fort Myers 33907
239-267-1905
trainweb.org

Shell Point Retirement Community
15101 Shell Point Blvd., Fort Myers 33908
239-466-1111
shellpoint.org

SIT BACK
AND BE ENTERTAINED

"Tonight's audience is our favorite audience! You're the best-looking and most intelligent, and I swear, I always say that," Robert Cacioppo, Florida Rep's producing artistic director, tells those attending each night's performance. *Wall Street Journal* drama critic Terry Teachout tells his reading audience, "Florida Rep is one of America's top repertory companies." The theater company has performed in the 1908 Arcade Theatre since 1998. Originally a vaudeville house, it later became a movie theater patronized by historic figures Thomas Edison and Henry Ford. The nonprofit professional Florida Rep presents nine productions each season, September through May, in its 393-seat main stage theater and 120-seat Artstage Studio Theatre. Florida Rep entertains with gut-busting comedies, Pulitzer Prize-winning plays, and traditional musicals. During the summer months, the theater is devoted to its education department.

2268 Bay St., Fort Myers 33901
239-332-4488
floridarep.org

TIP
Florida Rep's website offers tips on parking, dining, overnight stays, playing, and shopping in the area. Group pricing and discounts are listed.

ROCK OUT
AT LIVE TRIBUTE PERFORMANCES

The Stage Restaurant & Live Music hosts an unusual brand of musical dinner theater. It lines up entertainment from live music tribute bands to accompany dinner and dancing. The bands emulate "big name" performers such as The Beatles, The Rolling Stones, Lady Gaga, Fleetwood Mac, Abba, Neil Diamond, Cher, The Beach Boys, and the Eagles—to name a few of the headliners. Dinner includes a selection of entrées and dessert. A full cash bar mixes up adult libations to lubricate the dance moves. Show tickets include a cover charge, dinner, and guaranteed seating. Reservations can be made online or by calling.

9144 Bonita Beach Rd. SE, Bonita Springs 34135
239-405-8566
thestagebonita.com

TIP
Although The Stage does accept walk-ins, reservations are recommended during the peak tourism season—January through April— and holiday periods.

WALK THE WALKS
TO CELEBRATE THE ARTS

Free, public, self-guided monthly events fill the downtown Fort Myers River District with lively celebrations of the arts—both visual and musical. Art Walk coincides with opening exhibits at fourteen galleries on the first Friday evenings and Saturday daytimes of each month. Art lovers can meet the artists and watch live demonstrations. Music Walk brings the sounds of the community alive on the third Friday evening of the month as local and regional musicians line the streets along restaurants and shops. From jazz and blues to rock and roll, the many different genres vary from month to month. Street parking is free after 5 p.m. for participants, who come to eat, dance, shop, and enjoy the festive atmosphere.

Art Walk
Arts for ACT, 2265 First St., Fort Myers 33901
239-337-5050
fortmyersartwalk.com

Music Walk
River District Alliance, P.O. Box 1686, Fort Myers 33902
1-855-732-3836
fortmyersriverdistrictalliance.com

ENTERTAIN THE FAMILY
WITH COOL ACTIVITIES

While growing up and attending North Fort Myers High School, Mike Greenwell remembers the limited number of safe places where kids could find entertainment. After retiring from playing leftfield for the Boston Red Sox, he opened Mike Greenwell's Bat-A-Ball & Family Fun Park. The park encompasses batting cages, go-kart tracks, miniature golf, a fish-feeding dock, a paintball field, an arcade, and a playground. Another nearby venue, Sun Splash Family Waterpark, boasts fourteen acres of slides and pools. Highlights include Cape Fear, Fun-L-Tunnel, Zoom Flume, and the 457-foot Electric Slide & Power Surge. A Lazy River and Tot Spot allow for a gentler experience. As you head toward the beach, look for Zoomers Amusement Park, which has indoor and outdoor activities that will keep the family busy. It offers a roller coaster, go-karts, miniature golf, arcade games, bumper boats, and kiddie midway rides.

Mike Greenwell's Bat-A-Ball &
Family Fun Park
35 Pine Island Rd., Cape Coral 33909
239-574-4386
greenwellsfamilyfunpark.com

Sun Splash Family Waterpark
400 Santa Barbara Blvd.,
Cape Coral 33991
239-574-0558
sunsplashwaterpark.com

Zoomers Amusement Park
17455 Summerlin Rd., Fort Myers 33908
239-481-9666
zoomersamusementpark.com

APPRECIATE LIVE THEATER
AT BROADWAY PALM

In the early 1990s, the Prather family arrived in Fort Myers with plans to convert a grocery store into a successful dinner theater. More than two decades and hundreds of shows later, Broadway Palm has become the premier dinner theater in Southwest Florida. The facility includes a 450-seat dinner theater, a one-hundred-seat "black box" venue called the Off Broadway Palm Theatre, the 135-seat Royal Palm Room dining area, and a thirty-two-seat space just off the main lobby known as the Sabal Palm Room, which features revolving exhibits of local art. For productions from the blockbuster *Chicago* to children's theater, the Prathers audition actors in New York City and complete the cast with local talent. The venue also hosts concerts, community events, and philanthropic fundraisers.

1380 Colonial Blvd., Fort Myers 33907
239-278-4422
broadwaypalm.com

TIP
Groups of twenty or more can obtain a discount for theater productions.

ENJOY COMMUNITY ART
IN ALL FORMS

For local theater and gallery exhibitions, check the schedule at the Alliance for the Arts and BIG ARTS Sanibel Island. The Alliance, founded in 1975, serves as an umbrella organization for all the arts. Its ten-acre campus along the famed royal palm-lined McGregor Boulevard houses the twelve-thousand-square-foot William R. Frizzell Cultural Centre with public galleries hosting new exhibits each month. Added later, the 150-seat Claiborne and the 135-seat Ned Foulds Theatre, as well as the Margaret Morrow Frizzell Amphitheater, present theatrical productions including dramas, comedies, recitals, and concerts. Year-round, the Alliance hosts classes, workshops, and a GreenMarket. Out on the islands, BIG ARTS Sanibel Island features music, theater, and dance in the 132-seat BIG ARTS Strauss Theater, fine art exhibits in various galleries, and an indie film series in Schein Hall.

Alliance for the Arts
10091 McGregor Blvd.,
Fort Myers 33919
239-939-2787
artinlee.org

BIG ARTS Sanibel Island
900 Dunlop Rd., Sanibel 33957
239-395-0900
bigarts.org

TIP
Check the location of each event on the websites.

CHEER ON
YOUR CRAB

"They're off and hauling shell," yells Tim Jardas, crab race commissioner. Were you expecting "start your engines"? We are, after all, talking about the Captiva Island Crab Races, which have been held at 'Tween Waters Inn Island Resort & Spa for the last thirty-plus years. Most Monday and Thursday nights, everyone digs deep as the battle heats up to crown the winner of the hermit crab races. Two shows take place in the resort's Crow's Nest Bar & Grille: one for families at 6 p.m. and the adult version at 9 p.m. For an optional donation, spectators can name their crabs to enter into the running for fastest crab. Popular names include Speedy, Bob, Fred, Sandy Claws, and various superhero characters. When the final race ends, the winner splits the pot with the United Way as a donation to military veterans.

15951 Captiva Dr., Captiva 33924
239-472-5161
tween-waters.com

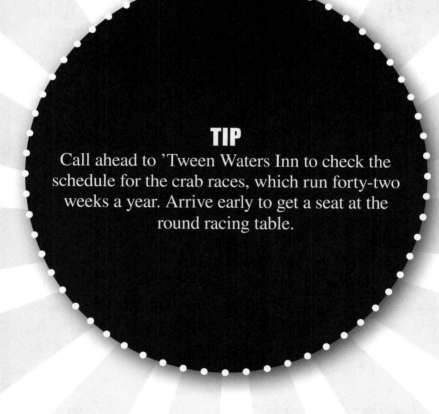

TIP

Call ahead to 'Tween Waters Inn to check the schedule for the crab races, which run forty-two weeks a year. Arrive early to get a seat at the round racing table.

IGNITE
THE MUSIC LOVER IN YOU
WITH TWO SYMPHONY ORCHESTRAS

The Southwest Florida Symphony (SWFLSO) has delighted audiences for more than fifty years with a professional concert orchestra. Each season, Maestro Nir Kabaretti and sixty-five world-class musicians perform a series of five Masterworks concerts, three Pops concerts, a Holiday Pops, and a Small Stage Symphonies series. Dr. Andrew Kurtz conducts a second orchestra—the Gulf Coast Symphony (GCS), which is the premier nonprofit community orchestra of Southwest Florida. This symphony presents a wide-ranging Classical Access and Symphonic Pops series during its October-through-June concert season. The GCS teams up with local theater and opera production companies to produce special events. Both symphonies present their events at the Barbara B. Mann Performing Arts Hall on the campus of Florida SouthWestern State College.

Southwest Florida Symphony
8290 College Pkwy.,
Fort Myers 33919
Box Office 239-418-1500
swflso.org

Gulf Coast Symphony
6314 Corporate Ct., #100,
Fort Myers 33919
239-277-1700, Box Office
239-481-4849
gulfcoastsymphony.org

TIP

The SWFLSO holds open rehearsals
throughout the year at the Riverside
Community Center. Student groups can contact
the symphony office at 239-418-0996.
The GCS offers 20 Days of Music, featuring more
than twenty free educational and community
engagement activities throughout Southwest
Florida in January and February.
Check the website for dates.

APPLAUD PROFESSIONAL PRODUCTIONS
AT BARBARA B. MANN PERFORMING ARTS HALL

Barbara B. Mann was awarded her Fort Myers High School diploma by Thomas Edison and once received flowers from Mina Edison following her starring role in a play. She dedicated her life to the arts, and so it was fitting that the Barbara B. Mann Performing Arts Hall paid homage to this local philanthropist when it opened in 1986 on the campus of today's Florida SouthWestern State College. The 1,859-seat hall hosts a schedule of national touring Broadway productions, prominent entertainers, dance performances, popular ensembles, and classical music concerts year-round. Massive productions such as *The Phantom of the Opera* as well as the technically challenging *Wicked* have played here. Check the website to see when your favorite musical, rock star, or comedian is in town. Seasonal and individual tickets are available. Parking is free.

13350 FSW Pkwy., Fort Myers 33919
239-489-3033, Box Office 239-481-4849
bbmannpah.com

TAKE TO THE SEAS
FOR A PIRATE ADVENTURE

Folklore has it that Spanish pirate José Gaspar lived around Pine Island Sound in the early 1800s. According to legend, he established headquarters on Sanibel Island (Santa Isybella), held his ransomed female prisoners on Captiva Island (Isla de las Captivas), and buried his treasure on Gasparilla Island. Today's buccaneers can get a taste of Gaspar's pirate lifestyle aboard *Pieces of Eight,* a sixty-five-foot replica of a Spanish galleon with all the rigging. The boat takes ninety-minute cruises out of Salty Sam's Marina into scenic Estero Bay. Modern-day pirates host daytime family cruises complete with face painting, games, prizes, pirate history, limbo dancing, and the hunt for treasure. Pirate grog and grub are available for purchase. Evening ARRRRRRGH-rated adult-only cruises are offered as well. Call for the schedule.

2500 Main St., Fort Myers Beach 33931
239-765-7272
floridapiratecruise.com

TIP
Turn out in your finest pirate attire for the annual Fort Myers Beach Pirate Festival, held each October.

CELEBRATE HERITAGE, SHELLS, AND MORE
AT LOCAL FESTIVALS

What started in Fort Myers as the three-day Edison Pageant of Light in 1938 has expanded to a three-week illumination of the life of prolific inventor Thomas A. Edison, who wintered in Fort Myers for many years. The current Edison Festival of Light attracts more than a half-million people annually to the myriad events, including arts and crafts, an inventors fair, an antique car show, a garden festival, and a junior parade. It culminates in one of the top five U.S. nighttime parades. Another top-rated event, the Sanibel Shell Fair & Show, began in 1937 on the porch of the Island Inn—the oldest inn on the island. Other festivals, from seafood to sand sculpting, offer a sampling of elements that define the area.

Edison Festival of Light
(January/February)
Throughout Fort Myers
239-334-2999
edisonfestival.org

Sanibel Shell Fair & Show (March)
2173 Periwinkle Way,
Sanibel 33957
239-472-2155
sanibelcommunityhouse.net

TIP
Edison paradegoers reserve their seats up to a month in advance by placing folding chairs and putting tape down on parade route sidewalks. Local courtesy respects these markers. Those arriving later to town can call the festival office for more seating options.

ArtFest Fort Myers (February)
1375 Monroe St., Fort Myers 33901
239-768-3602
artfestfortmyers.com

Burrowing Owl Festival (February)
Rotary Park Environmental Center, 5505 Rose Garden Rd.,
Cape Coral 33914
ccfriendsofwildlife.org

Fort Myers Beach Shrimp Festival & Parade (February or March)
Fort Myers Beach 33931
239-463-6986
fortmyersbeachshrimpfestival.com

MangoMania Tropical Fruit Festival (July)
Pine Island 33922
239-283-0888
mangomaniafl.net

Island Hopper Songwriter Fest (September/October)
Captiva Island, Fort Myers Beach, Fort Myers
239-338-3500
islandhopperfest.com

Ding Darling Days (October)
J.N. "Ding" Darling National Wildlife Refuge,
1 Wildlife Dr., Sanibel 33957
239-472-1100
dingdarlingsociety.org/dingdarlingdays.php

Coconut Festival (November)
Sun Splash Waterpark, 400 Santa Barbara Blvd., Cape Coral 33991
239-573-3121
cocofest.com

American Sand Sculpting Championship (November)
South end of Fort Myers Beach 33931
239-454-7500
fmbsandsculpting.com

Holiday Nights (December)
Edison & Ford Winter Estates, 2350 McGregor Blvd., Fort Myers 33901
239-334-7419
edisonfordwinterestates.org

HASTEN IN,
THE MUSIC'S GREAT

As the waves gently roll in onto the shores of Sanibel Island each March, so do the classical notes of the annual Sanibel Music Festival. Musician and impresario Marilyn Lauriente started the festival in the 1980s. It has featured such groups as the Emerson String Quartet, the Julliard String Quartet, the American String Quartet, the Pacifica Quartet, and the Pražák Quartet. Renowned pianists who have performed at the festival include Olga Kern, Wu Han, Orion Weiss, Joyce Yang, Jon Nakamatsu, and Ruth Laredo. The Opera Theater of Connecticut has even produced a special staging. The festival's "Save March for Music" season offers seven concerts with piano, chamber music, recital, and vocal ensembles. All programs begin at 8 p.m. Check the website for performances.

Sanibel Congregational Church, 2050 Periwinkle Way, Sanibel Island 33957
239-344-7025
sanibelmusicfestival.org

MEET THE TALENT
BEHIND THE HITS

Each fall, musicians and music fans assemble to exchange notes at the annual Island Hopper Songwriter Fest in Southwest Florida. This free, ten-day festival marries the area's stunning barrier islands with star-studded performances. Indoor and outdoor concerts take place on Captiva Island, on Fort Myers Beach, and in the historic Fort Myers River District. In small, intimate venues, the festival offers music lovers the opportunity to hear the stories behind the songs. Tickets are available on a limited basis for the more than one hundred performances. While not all the songwriters' names are well known, the performers who sing and record their work have included such artists as George Strait, the Dixie Chicks, Bonnie Raitt, Trisha Yearwood, Cher, and Art Garfunkel.

Lee County Visitor & Convention Bureau
Locations throughout Lee County
239-338-3500
www.islandhopperfest.com

TIP
Hotel packages are usually available for the festival.
Check the website for details.

CATCH THE BIG SHOWS
AT GERMAIN ARENA

Besides rocking Everblades hockey fans in the fall and winter, Germain Arena entertains year-round with a wide variety of big-venue events. Since opening in 1998, it has hosted NHL, NBA, USBL, and arena football games. With a seating capacity of seven thousand-plus, Germain holds more than three hundred different events a year—from Stars on Ice, Disney On Ice, and WWE wrestling to Jeff Dunham, the Boston Pops, and Lord of the Dance. Headline concerts have featured Cher, Elton John, Alan Jackson, Guns N' Roses, Def Leppard, Sting, Keith Urban, Eric Church, the Zac Brown Band, and Toby Keith. The venue has a sports pub, restaurant, suites, pro shop, and two recreational ice rinks.

11000 Everblades Pkwy., Estero 33928
239-948-7825
germainarena.com

TIP
Even though this is Florida, public ice skating is available year-round. Check skateeverblades.com for schedule.

TAKE A COOL BREAK WITH MUSIC
ALONG THE WATERFRONT

As the breeze comes off the water, palm trees sway, and the live music kicks in, sit back and relax at one of several waterfront establishments. Bert's Bar & Grill, a casual place on Matlacha Pass, features seafood and local music. The Cottage Beach Bar & Gulfshore Grill, another longtime favorite, sits directly on the Gulf of Mexico in Fort Myers Beach. The beach bar serves cocktails, a full menu, gorgeous sunsets, and a lively music setting. Also popular is Doc Ford's Rum Bar & Grille, located on Matanzas Harbor and excelling in seafood, South American flavors, fruity drinks, and live entertainment. Other nearby restaurant/nightspots include Nervous Nellie's and Parrot Key Caribbean Grill at Salty Sam's Marina, which are family restaurants with food, cocktails, and special musical events.

Bert's Bar & Grill
Matlacha Pass Aquatic Preserve, 4271 Pine Island Rd.,
Matlacha 33993
239-282-3232
bertsbar.com

The Cottage Beach Bar & Gulfshore Grill
1250 Estero Blvd., Fort Myers Beach 33931
239-765-5440
gulfshoregrill.com

Doc Ford's Rum Bar & Grille
708 Fisherman's Wharf, Fort Myers Beach 33931
239-765-9660
docfords.com/ft-myers-beach

Nervous Nellie's
1131 First St., Fort Myers Beach 33931
239-463-8077
nervousnellies.net

Parrot Key Caribbean Grill
Estero Bay Aquatic Preserve, 2500 Main St.,
Fort Myers Beach 33931
239-463-3257
myparrotkey.com

Photo Credit:
Courtesy of Lee County Visitor & Convention Bureau

SPORTS AND RECREATION

TAKE A GANDER
AT THE NORTH AMERICAN
MIGRATION FLYWAY

Early-twentieth-century Pulitzer Prize-winning cartoonist and pioneer environmentalist Jay Norwood Darling was a Sanibel Island hero. He blocked the development of sensitive land and encouraged President Harry Truman to sign an executive order creating the Sanibel National Wildlife Refuge (NWR) in 1945. The refuge was later named for him. The 6,400-acre J.N. "Ding" Darling NWR features footpaths lined by native habitat that shelters wildlife, winding paddling trails, and a four-mile scenic drive. Mangrove-laden waterways provide opportunities to view roseate spoonbills, great blue herons, white pelicans, and the myriad species that make their way along the North American Migration Flyway. Away from the water, inland birds such as bald eagles and wood storks take refuge among the nation's largest stand of bald cypress trees at the Audubon Corkscrew Swamp Sanctuary. Both locations are important stops on the Great Florida Birding & Wildlife Trail.

J.N. "Ding" Darling
National Wildlife Refuge
1 Wildlife Dr., Sanibel 33957
239-472-1100
fws.gov/dingdarling

Audubon Corkscrew
Swamp Sanctuary
375 Sanctuary Rd. W.,
Naples 34120
239-348-9151
corkscrew.audubon.org

TIP

The Great Florida Birding & Wildlife Trail is composed of 510 premier wildlife-viewing areas. For a complete list of these areas in Southwest Florida, visit floridabirdingtrail.com/trail/trail-sections/ south-section/.

KICK OFF
YOUR FLIP-FLOPS

Many people think of the beach as their happy place. So, with fifty miles of white sand beach and 590 miles of shoreline, the area has a lot to make people smile. A number of the beaches have been recognized by top media publications and travel organizations for various attributes: Bowman's Beach on Sanibel for shelling and peace, Lovers Key State Park for romance, Alison Hagerup Beach on Captiva's north end for beachcombing and sunsets, and Cayo Costa State Park for seclusion. There are even beaches for our furry friends, namely Dog Beach. Along with the beaches, more than one hundred parks and preserves cradle twenty thousand-plus acres of environmentally significant land for recreation purposes. So go ahead and play outside!

Lee County Parks & Recreation
3410 Palm Beach Blvd.,
Fort Myers 33916
239-533-7275
leegov.com/parks

City of Sanibel
800 Dunlop Rd., Sanibel 33957
239-472-3700
mysanibel.com;
search for beaches and parks

TIP
Seventy-three public beach accesses run from Boca Grande south to Bonita Beach. Parking is free at some of the smaller accesses, but watch for signage because the main beach accesses and state parks charge a fee. Also, many of the areas have no vehicular parking, with pedestrian/bike access only.

MAKE A DIFFERENCE
TO SAVE WILDLIFE

One small creature and one caring woman made a difference on Sanibel starting in 1968. After a car injured a royal tern on the causeway, islander Shirley Walter took the bird home to nurse it. Friends including Dr. Phyllis Douglass stepped in to help as other injured and orphaned animals came to live under Shirley's care. That year the volunteers answered five hundred distress calls, and the Clinic for the Rehabilitation of Wildlife (CROW) was born. After incorporation as a nonprofit in 1972, growing pains led the clinic to move to its current ten-acre site in 1981. The patient load has grown to more than four thousand annually. For its fortieth anniversary in 2008, CROW opened a state-of-the-art hospital and visitor education center with displays, interactive exhibits, live patient videos, wildlife presentations, and special events.

3883 Sanibel-Captiva Rd., Sanibel 33957
239-472-3644
crowclinic.org

TIP
If you come across an abandoned creature,
here's some helpful information:
crowclinic.org/articles/if-you-care-leave-it-there.

EXPLORE NATURAL WONDERS
BY FOOT AND BY WHEEL

In 1996, Lee County residents voted to tax themselves to preserve public land for nonintrusive use, creating myriad hiking and biking opportunities. Among the preserved areas are the 1.2-mile boardwalk at the Six Mile Cypress Slough Preserve and the two-mile Indigo Trail at J.N. "Ding" Darling National Wildlife Refuge, where visitors can spot waterfowl, fish, and gators. To travel through a nature preserve, try the Sanibel-Captiva Conservation Foundation trail. For a coastal experience, hike and bike through Lovers Key State Park. At Crew Corkscrew Marsh, meander the trails through pine flat woods, oak, and palm hammocks, where wood storks and red-shouldered hawks soar. Visitors to the Caloosahatchee Regional Park will discover scrublands and wetlands along the river. The north side of the park is open to mountain bikes and equestrian riders. There are even shell paths at this park that assist those in wheelchairs in exploring nature.

TIP

There are sixty miles of marked and maintained trails as well as sixteen miles of primitive trails in Lee County for hiking.
More than 195 miles of paths are available for cyclists.

Six Mile Cypress Slough Preserve
7751 Penzance Blvd., Fort Myers 33906
239-533-7556
leegov.com/parks/parks

J.N. "Ding" Darling National Wildlife Refuge
1 Wildlife Dr., Sanibel 33957
239-472-1100
fws.gov/dingdarling

Sanibel-Captiva Conservation Foundation
3333 Sanibel-Captiva Rd., Sanibel 33957
239-472-2329
sccf.org

Lovers Key State Park
8700 Estero Blvd., Fort Myers Beach 33931
239-463-4588
floridastateparks.org/loverskey

Crew Corkscrew Marsh
23998 Corkscrew Rd., Estero 33928
239-657-2253
crewtrust.org

Caloosahatchee Regional Park
19130 N. River Rd., Alva 33920
239-694-0398
leegov.com/parks/parks

CAMP
AT HISTORIC SITES

The Red Coconut RV Park is one of the first, and one of only a few, campgrounds located on oceanfront beaches in existence today in Florida. The land, plotted in 1898, officially became a trailer park in the 1920s. In 1932, owner Virgil Voorhis built a pavilion on the property that was used as the first voting precinct and a spiritual gathering place before there was a church on the island. Thomas Edison's wife, Mina, would also hold ladies' teas there. At times, it served as a bingo hall to raise money for the island's first school. Several owners later, Tom and Fran Myers keep up the park's legacy. Red Coconut has sixty RV sites on the white, powdery sand. The other 190 sites sit across the street on the park side of the property. For tent camping, try Caloosahatchee Regional Park, Cayo Costa State Park, Koreshan State Park, and Periwinkle Park.

TIP
For more beach history, visit the Fort Myers Beach Historical Society or log on to esteroislandhistoricsociety.org.

Red Coconut RV Park
Estero Blvd., Fort Myers Beach 33931
239-463-7200
redcoconut.com

Caloosahatchee Regional Park
19130 N. River Rd., Alva 33920
239-694-0398
leegov.com/parks/parks

Cayo Costa State Park
Island south of Boca Grande (remote)
941-964-0375
floridastateparks.org/cayocosta

Koreshan State Park
3800 Corkscrew Rd., Estero 33928
239-992-0311
floridastateparks.org/koreshan

Periwinkle Park
1119 Periwinkle Way, Sanibel 33957
239-472-1433
sanibelcamping.com

BECOME
WILDLIFE WISE

Environmental education is crucial in a fragile subtropical island setting such as Southwest Florida. To learn more about the local environment and its inhabitants, visit the area's nature and science centers. Calusa Nature Center and Planetarium comprises a museum, three nature trails, a planetarium, a butterfly house, a bird aviary, a gift shop, and picnic areas on its 105-acre site. The planetarium offers a glimpse of the constellations and hosts special events, including laser shows. You can find another butterfly house out on the islands at the Sanibel-Captiva Conservation Foundation, which educates visitors about the conservation of coastal habitats and aquatic resources through displays, trails, and programs at its Nature Center and Bailey Homestead Preserve. In Fort Myers, The Butterfly Estates is home to a 3,600-square-foot glass conservatory. Its Florida Native Butterfly Society is dedicated to butterfly protection and preservation.

Calusa Nature Center
and Planetarium
3450 Ortiz Ave., Fort Myers 33905
239-275-3435
calusanature.org

Sanibel-Captiva
Conservation Foundation
3333 Sanibel-Captiva Rd.,
Sanibel 33957
239-472-2329
sccf.org

The Butterfly Estates
1815 Fowler St., Fort Myers 33901
239-690-2359
thebutterflyestates.com

STOP, DROP, AND STOOP
FOR SEASHELLS

When Anne Morrow Lindbergh visited Captiva Island, gathering shells and thoughts to pen her famous 1955 book, *Gift from the Sea,* she wrote: "The beach was covered with beautiful shells ... I couldn't even walk head up looking out to sea, for fear of missing something precious at my feet." Today avid collectors comb shorelines in a posture known as the "Sanibel Stoop," looking for—among other prizes—the illusive brown-speckled junonia. These beaches are tops in the world of shelling. The Bailey-Matthews National Shell Museum on Sanibel attests to the area's reputation. The island also hosts the annual Shell Festival each March.

Bailey-Matthews National
Shell Museum
3075 Sanibel-Captiva Rd.,
Sanibel 33957, 239-395-2233
shellmuseum.org

Sanibel Shell Festival
Sanibel Community House,
2173 Periwinkle Way,
Sanibel 33957, 239-472-2155
sanibelcommunityhouse.net

Captiva Cruises
11401 Rosse Ln.,
Captiva 33924, 239-472-5300
captivacruises.com

FUN FACT
In 2012, Sanibel Island set the Guinness World Record for largest scavenger hunt, with more than one thousand people simultaneously performing the Sanibel Stoop in search of seashells.

EXPERIENCE A DAYTRIP ADVENTURE
TO THE FAMED EVERGLADES

People come from around the globe to explore the Florida Everglades, a short daytrip from the Fort Myers/Sanibel area. Nature lovers can book an all-encompassing nine-hour eco-tour guided by naturalists at Everglades Day Safari. The day starts with a drive to Lake Trafford for a sixty-minute airboat ride to see alligators and birds. Next, it's off to the Big Cypress National Preserve for more wildlife watching, followed by a midday lunch stop in Everglades City, where, if you dare, alligator appetizers are the star of the menu. Then, on to the historic Smallwood Store for a sixty-minute mangrove cruise to look for dolphins, river otters, turtles, and the endangered West Indian manatee. A nature walk on a 1.6-mile boardwalk through the Fakahatchee Strand State Preserve concludes your adventure.

14900 S. Tamiami Trl., Fort Myers 33912
239-472-1559
ecosafari.com

TIP

Adventurers should wear light clothing, comfortable shoes, sunscreen, and a hat. Don't forget your camera. Tour guides provide a rain poncho and bug spray if needed. This is an adventure—the tour runs rain or shine seven days a week.

Other day adventures:

Key West Express
High-speed passenger ferry service from Fort Myers
Beach to Key West. Go for the day or stay overnight.
1200 Main St., Fort Myers Beach 33931
239-463-5733
keywestexpress.net

**Naples, Marco Island,
Everglades Convention & Visitors Bureau**
Walk the one-thousand-foot Naples Pier,
then visit restaurants, shops, and cultural attractions to
complete the day.
2660 N. Horseshoe Dr., #105, Naples 34104
1-800-688-3600
paradisecoast.com

DIVE INTO THE HISTORY
OF COASTAL WATERS

Once home to hundreds of servicemen, the WWII warship USS *Mohawk* now provides shelter for marine life as a living artificial reef twenty-eight nautical miles off Sanibel's coast. It has become a favorite hangout for humongous whale sharks, giant goliath grouper, and other intriguing sea life. Divers discover the thrill of the ship as well as the sea creatures forty-five to ninety feet under the water's surface. The one-hundred-foot *Ultimate Getaway,* out of Fort Myers Beach, takes divers to the *Mohawk*. Other dive sites include a four-hundred-foot freighter with its current crew of tarpon, barracuda, reef fish, and soft corals west of Boca Grande; a Honduran freighter off Fort Myers; and a railcar off Boca Grande.

Ultimate Getaway
18450 San Carlos Blvd., Fort Myers Beach 33931
239-466-0466
ultimategetaway.net

TIP
Check out the artificial reefs program at leereefs.org.

VIEW WILDLIFE
IN A PRISTINE ENVIRONMENT

The fragile, pristine environment of Southwest Florida provides an ideal "classroom" for learning about the area's various ecosystems and their inhabitants. Start your education in the million-plus acres of local nature sanctuaries. Paddle, cruise, bike, and hike through the subtropical habitat. The Sanibel Sea School takes families on outings to discover life in the sea. Captiva Cruises and Adventures in Paradise also lead wildlife-watching excursions and shelling tours to the outer islands. In Fort Myers, Pure Florida specializes in eco-tours with certified master naturalists who are experts in wildlife, bird watching, and natural history. Tarpon Bay Explorers on Sanibel Island excels at naturalist-guided kayak and sea life tours through the J.N. "Ding" Darling National Wildlife Refuge. Nearby Babcock Wilderness Adventures offers eco-tours through the Telegraph Cypress Swamp to see panthers, alligators, deer, and wild turkey.

Sanibel Sea School
414 Lagoon Dr., Sanibel 33957
239-472-8585
sanibelseaschool.org

Captiva Cruises
11401 Andy Rosse Ln., Captiva 33924
239-472-5300
captivacruises.com

Adventures in Paradise
14341 Port Comfort Rd., G Dock, Fort Myers 33908
239-472-8443
adventureinparadiseinc.com

Pure Florida
The Marina at Edison Ford, 2360 W. First St.,
Fort Myers 33901
239-919-2965
purefl.com

Tarpon Bay Explorers
900 Tarpon Bay Rd., Sanibel 33957
239-472-8900
tarponbayexplorers.com

Babcock Wilderness Adventures
8000 SR 31, Punta Gorda 33982
941-637-0551
babcockwilderness.com

HAVE A BLAST
AT SPRING TRAINING BASEBALL

Baseball and Southwest Florida go way back together. In 1896, the Philadelphia Athletics played the first organized game in Fort Myers. The team began training here in 1925 and was followed by the Cleveland Indians, Pittsburgh Pirates, and Kansas City Royals. The Twins arrived in 1991 and the Red Sox in 1993. Each February equipment trucks head south. Three weeks later, the catchers and pitchers are warming up, with the remainder of the team not far behind. Games start as February turns to March for Major League Baseball's Grapefruit League. Red Sox Nation and Twins fans converge on Fort Myers each year for afternoon and evening games at JetBlue Park/Fenway South and Hammond Stadium/CenturyLink Sports Complex, respectively.

Boston Red Sox
11500 Fenway South Dr.,
Fort Myers 33913
239-334-4700
redsox.com

Minnesota Twins
14100 Six Mile Cypress Pkwy.,
Fort Myers 33912
612-33-TWINS (8-9467)
twinsbaseball.com

FUN FACT
Each major league team has gone on to win the World Series after moving here for spring training.

TIPS

Check websites for spring training ticket sales, since they go fast and most games sell out. Stand near the dugouts before games to secure player autographs. The Class A Fort Myers Miracle, an affiliate of the Minnesota Twins, plays here from April through the beginning of September.

Fort Myers Miracle
14400 6 Mile Cypress Pkwy.,
Fort Myers 33912
239-768-4210
milb.com

COOL OFF
AT A HOT HOCKEY MATCH

Professional ice hockey played in Florida? While the outside temperatures might be hot, so is the action on the ice when the Florida Everblades play ECHL AA hockey at Germain Arena from October through April. An affiliate of the Carolina Hurricanes, the team formed in 1998. Since then, the Everblades have only missed the playoffs once and have played for the Kelly Cup three times, winning in 2012. One of the most popular games each year, the Teddy Bear Toss takes place in December. Fans bring a new teddy bear or stuffed animal to the game. When the Everblades score their first goal, they toss the plush toys onto the ice to celebrate. Thousands of teddy bears and stuffed animals get collected and distributed to local children's charities across Southwest Florida for the holiday season.

11000 Everblades Pkwy., Estero 33928
239-948-7825
floridaeverblades.com

PADDLE THE
GREAT CALUSA BLUEWAY

Paddling on the waters of the Gulf of Mexico and its tributaries dates back thousands of years to when the Calusa natives inhabited Southwest Florida. They were the inspiration for the name of the Great Calusa Blueway, a 190-mile marked paddling trail, which meanders these same waterways. The trail is divided into three main sections. The Estero Bay part covers the waterways from Bonita Springs to Fort Myers Beach. The Pine Island Sound and Matlacha Pass segment includes the barrier islands from Gasparilla to Sanibel as well as inner islands such as Pine Island. The third encompasses the Caloosahatchee River and its tributaries—from the Gulf to the small community of Alva. Calm, shallow waters make these waterways a natural for novices. Along the way you may eye manatees, dolphins, rays, herons, egrets, otters, and turtles, as well as paddle through mangrove caves.

Great Calusa Blueway
Lee County Parks & Recreation
3410 Palm Beach Blvd., Fort Myers 33916
239-533-7275
calusablueway.com

TIP
The Blueway website is a great resource for finding outfitters to safely explore the waterways.

REEL IN
THE BIG ONE

Fishing the waters off Fort Myers and Sanibel offers an unrivaled experience thanks to massive shallow grass flats, brackish and saltwater opportunities, bountiful access, and trophy game that anglers from around the world seek. The passes between islands are home to the largest U.S. migration of tarpon each summer. Offshore reefs and the Gulf of Mexico bring spearfishing challenges, while a huge concentration of protected goliath grouper adds to the sport. Sandy shores provide pier and beach fishing for flounder and crafty snook. Other sought-after catches include redfish, seatrout, cobia, snapper, and tripletail. No wonder *Field & Stream* magazine named the area among the twenty-five hottest fishing spots in North America. Tournaments happen regularly, including the Calusa Blueway Kayak Fishing Tournament. For your first time in local waters, consider a charter captain with local knowledge. Marinas and bait shops can help with contacts. Here are some suggestions to get started.

Fly Fishing
Capt. Mike Rehr
239-472-3308
captflyrod.com

Near Shore/Back Bay Fishing
Capt. Mark Westra
239-872-2962
flattopcharters.com

Offshore Fishing
Capt. Ozzie Fischer
239-872-8515
bayfischer@comcast.net

Adventures in Paradise
14341 Port Comfort Rd., Fort Myers 33908
239-472-8443
adventureinparadiseinc.com

Getaway Marina
18400 San Carlos Blvd., Fort Myers Beach 33931
239-466-3600
getawaymarina.com

Pure Florida – Fort Myers
2360 W. First St., Fort Myers 33901
239-919-2965
purefortmyers.com

GET TEED OFF
IN NATURE

Ranging from historic to amazing, the year-round golf scene in the Fort Myers area lends itself to professionals as well as amateurs. Take, for instance, the Fort Myers Country Club. Donald Ross designed the course in 1917, and Thomas Edison and Henry Ford played it in the '20s. Today players can walk this eighteen-hole, 6,414-yard course. Golfers seeking a bigger challenge play the eighteen-hole, 6,478-yard Raymond Floyd Raptor Bay Golf Club at the Hyatt Regency Coconut Point Resort and Spa. In its lush setting among the pines and palms, the course was the first in the world to be certified by Audubon International as a Gold Signature Sanctuary. Don't be surprised, while aiming to score a birdie, if a bald eagle flies overhead. For natural settings, the Jack Nicklaus Signature Course at Old Corkscrew Golf Club tops the leaderboard. The eighteen-hole, 7,400-yard course is Audubon certified and surrounded by mature oaks, pines, cypress trees, lakes, prairie grass, wetlands, and wildlife.

Fort Myers Country Club
3591 McGregor Blvd.,
Fort Myers 33901
239-321-7488
cityftmyers.com

Raptor Bay Golf Club
23001 Coconut Point Resort Dr.,
Bonita Springs 34134
239-390-4600
raptorbaygolfclub.com

Old Corkscrew Golf Course
17320 Corkscrew Rd., Estero 33928
239-949-4700
oldcorkscrew.com

ISLAND HOP
FOR DISCOVERY

More than one hundred coastal and barrier islands, a subtropical climate, and calm Gulf waters make for ideal island hopping by boat to destinations a car can't reach. Each island claims its own character, providing sunsets, shelling, dining, and opportunities for exploring. Climb aboard Captiva Cruises to Cabbage Key Inn and Restaurant, a 1930s-era home-turned-inn sitting atop a Calusa shell mound. Or travel to Useppa Island—once home to advertising executive Barron Collier, who hosted guests from movie stars to presidents, the island was later the site of training for the Bay of Pigs Invasion. For a natural experience, take a ferry with Tropic Star to Cayo Costa State Park for beachcombing. Or visit Boca Grande on Gasparilla Island—although you can reach it by car, a boat trip is the way to go. Glimpse where Katharine Hepburn escaped Hollywood to relax and the Du Ponts and Rockefellers once built winter homes.

Captiva Cruises
McCarthy's Marina, 11401
Andy Rosse Ln., Captiva 33924
239-472-5300
captivacruises.com

Tropic Star of Pine Island
16498 Tortuga St., Bokeelia 33922
239-283-0015
tropicstaradventures.com

TIP
While Useppa Island is private, day cruises allow access. For island hopping, water taxis are available at marinas, or hire a charter and captain familiar with the shallow waters and sandbars to gain access to other islands.

ENCOUNTER ENDANGERED MANATEES
IN A NON-CAPTIVE SETTING

Every fall and winter, manatee lovers of yore would drive east on SR 80 and pull off onto the shoulder, park, and then walk to the canal by the power plant to see these beloved marine mammals. County and power plant officials agreed that this was an accident waiting to happen. With the go-ahead from both parties and tourist tax dollars to fund the project, the only thing missing was the maintenance. A group of high school students stepped forward to volunteer, and thus Manatee Park opened in 1996. The seventeen-acre site along the Orange River is home to hundreds of endangered West Indian manatees that congregate there between November and March, when water temperatures in the Gulf and the rivers drop. This non-captive warm-water refuge provides a "manatee spa" and great wildlife viewing from three observation decks with interpretive naturalists on site.

10901 SR 80 (Palm Beach Blvd.), Fort Myers 33905
239-690-5030
leegov.com/parks/parks

LEARN A NEW SKILL
ON VACATION

Sailing brought Doris and Steve Colgate together. In the '60s, she was working at *Yachting* magazine. Steve was starting the Offshore Sailing School and competing in the America's Cup and the Olympics. She wanted to learn to sail. He needed help running his business while racing. It has worked well: fifty-plus years later they are still jointly operating a top-notch sailing school, which has graduated more than 140,000 sailors. Headquartered in Fort Myers, Offshore Sailing has six locations: Captiva Island, Fort Myers Beach, and St. Petersburg in Florida; and two in the British Virgin Islands. Offshore's courses range from Learn to Sail to Live Aboard and other sail and powerboat certifications. The Colgates partner with the resorts where they dock, so you can learn to sail while enjoying a resort vacation.

Offshore Sailing School
16731 McGregor Blvd., Ste. 110,
Fort Myers 33908
239-454-1700
offshoresailing.com

Pink Shell Beach Resort & Marina
275 Estero Blvd.,
Fort Myers Beach 33931
888-222-7465
pinkshell.com

South Seas Island Resort
5400 Plantation Rd., Captiva 33924
239-472-5111
southseas.com

The Westin Cape Coral Resort
at Marina Village
5951 Silver King Blvd.,
Cape Coral 33914
239-541-5000
westincapecoral.com

SEEK OUT
THE BIG THREE

In Southwest Florida, wildlife watchers seek to check the West Indian manatee, dolphin, and alligator off their list of sightings. Where are the best places to find them? Endangered manatees in the wild congregate at Manatee Park, a non-captive warm-water refuge with optimum viewing November through March, when the Gulf temperature drops. The Atlantic bottlenose dolphin frolics in the Gulf, back bays, estuaries, and even canals at times. Estero Bay, Florida's first aquatic preserve, founded in 1966, has one of the largest populations of dolphins, thanks to a huge food supply. And alligators, once endangered, now frequent freshwater rivers, lakes, ponds, and sometimes golf course water hazards. One place to see them in large numbers is Babcock Ranch, which offers swamp buggy tours through the Telegraph Cypress Swamp.

Manatee Park
10901 Palm
Beach Blvd.,
Fort Myers 33905
239-690-5030
leegov.com/parks

Estero Bay
Aquatic Preserve
700-1 Fisherman's Wharf,
Fort Myers Beach 33931
239-530-1001
dep.state.fl.us/coastal/sites/estero/

Babcock Wilderness
Adventures
8000 SR 31, Punta
Gorda 33982
941-637-0551
babcockwilderness.com

TIP
Never feed wildlife and keep a safe distance away while enjoying nature. Feeding alligators is punishable by a fee of up to $500.

PRESERVE TODAY
FOR FUTURE GENERATIONS

Conservation and preservation are a big part of the Fort Myers/ Sanibel area's ethic. Nonprofit organizations such as the Sanibel-Captiva Conservation Foundation (SCCF) monitor the waterways to help them stay healthy. Adopt a Road, Adopt a Beach, and Adopt an Island to keep the environment clean and natural for wildlife. Nonprofit groups work to save everything from manatees to seashells. One such group, Turtle Time, has been active since its founding by Eve Haverfield in the late '80s. The state-permitted organization monitors sea turtles from Bunche Beach in Fort Myers south to Bonita Beach. During "Lights Out for Turtles," May 1 through October 31, individuals walk the beaches to observe the nesting and hatching of endangered loggerhead and green sea turtles. Residents and visitors participate by turning lights off along the beach so as to not confuse the hatchlings enroute to the sea.

Turtle Time, Inc.
P.O. Box 2621, Fort Myers Beach 33931
239-481-5566
turtletime.org

TIP
People can participate with Turtle Time by emailing a request to witness the release of rescued hatchlings to eve@turtletime.org.

"SEAS" THE DAY
FOR EXCITEMENT AND RECREATION

Don your swimsuit and grab your favorite sports gear—whatever that may be. Some will reach for their fishing poles and head to the beach, pier, or bridge. Others will load up their kayaks, canoes, and paddleboards, heading for the back bays, rivers, and estuaries. Windsurfers, kiteboarders, and parasailers hit the gulf to catch air. Jet skiers and jet packers go for extreme adventure. Those who don't have their own equipment can find water sports concessions on Fort Myers Beach, on Bonita Beach, at Lovers Key State Park, at Tarpon Bay Recreation Area, and at local resorts. To find diving, fishing, and boating charters, contact dive shops, bait shops, and marinas.

Holiday Water Sports
239-765-4386
200 Estero Blvd., Fort Myers Beach 33931
holidaywatersportsfmb.com

Lovers Key Adventures/Nature Recreation Management
8700 Estero Blvd., Fort Myers Beach 33931
239-463-4588
loverskeyadventures.com

Tarpon Bay Explorers
900 Tarpon Bay Rd., Sanibel 33957
239-472-8900
tarponbayexplorers.com

CULTURE AND HISTORY

SEEK INSPIRATION
AT THE EDISON & FORD WINTER ESTATES

Find inspiration when you enter the riverfront estates of former residents Thomas A. Edison and his best friend and next-door neighbor, Henry Ford. The estates, on the National Register of Historic Places, are steeped in a rich history unique to the area. They have hosted some of the most prominent people of a bygone era: aviator Charles Lindbergh, businessman Harvey Firestone, and former president Herbert Hoover, to name a few. Take a step into the past when you peek into Edison's 1886 home and guesthouse, and then pass through his laboratory, where he experimented with plants from his botanical garden. You can make the short walk through Friendship Gate to Ford's 1916 home before perusing the gardens. Across the street, the museum contains Edison's myriad inventions and an assortment of rare antique automobiles. Return visitors may want to check out the specialty tours for the gardens and the river cruises.

2350 McGregor Blvd., Fort Myers 33901
239-334-7419
efwefla.org

TIP
Special events run throughout the year. Holiday Nights features themed decorations and millions of lights. Edison would be proud.

STEP INTO
A CATTLEMAN'S MANSION

For a glimpse of Fort Myers's cow-town roots—when a muddy trail provided access for cattle down McGregor Boulevard to the Punta Rassa docks—take a tour of the Burroughs Home & Gardens. John Murphy, a cattleman from Montana, built and lived in the 6,200-foot Georgian Revival mansion on the Caloosahatchee River. Today, actors portraying Mona and Jettie Burroughs, the privileged daughters of a wealthy businessman who purchased the home in 1918, re-create a living history. The Burroughses hosted many of the era's social events, entertaining the Edisons, Fords, and Firestones, among others. Antiques and historical artifacts fill the home, with its eleven-foot ceilings, Palladian windows, pine floors, oak fireplaces, and grand staircase. Listed on the National Register of Historic Places in 1984, it is often the scene of weddings.

2505 First St., Fort Myers 33901
239-337-0706
burroughshome.com

TIP
Tours are offered several days a week. Call for the schedule.

VIEW EARLY DAYS
IN FORT MYERS

Because of a hurricane during the Seminole War in the 1840s, Fort Dulaney had to be relocated from the mouth of the Caloosahatchee upriver to a spot that would later be named after Seminole War hero Colonel Abraham C. Myers. The new town of Fort Myers was incorporated in 1885. McGregor Boulevard was but a dirt road for cattle back then. Cowmen herded them along the dusty trail to the Punta Rassa docks to be loaded onto barges headed to Cuba. Early resident Thomas Edison had the idea to bring royal palm trees from Cuba to line McGregor Boulevard in 1907, which is why Fort Myers is known as the "City of Palms." A depiction of early history can be found in a brick courtyard outside the federal courthouse. A one-hundred-foot mural composed of one-inch mosaic tiles depicts contributions made by Florida Indians and African Americans, as well as the days of cattlemen and railroads.

Fort Myers: An Alternative History mural
2167 First St., Fort Myers 33901
artswfl.com

TIP
Historians believe that the Battle of Fort Myers, which was fought over cattle on February 20, 1865, was the southernmost battle of the Civil War.

SIFT THROUGH TIME
AT RANDELL RESEARCH CENTER

Col. Donald Randell knew there was something historically significant about the land he purchased on Pine Island in 1968. He hoped that someday experts would excavate and record the findings. In the mid-'90s, the colonel and his wife donated fifty-three acres to the University of Florida to use as an archeological research and education center about the Calusa Indians and the environment they lived in. The Calusa lived here until they died out in the mid-1700s. Well-preserved artifacts, hand-carved canals, and high mounds filled with shells left over from their diet of discarded seafood indicate a town that was their home for more than 1,500 years. Today visitors can walk the seven-tenths-of-a-mile Calusa Heritage Trail marked with interpretive signage to connect with this Indian culture of the past.

13810 Waterfront Dr., Pineland 33922
239-283-2062
floridamuseum.ufl.edu/rrc/

TIP
Contact the center if you wish to participate in an archeological dig.

DIG INTO
HISTORY

The oldest standing structure on Estero Island (aka Fort Myers Beach), Mound House was built in 1906 atop a two-thousand-year-old Calusa Indian shell mound. The Ellis and Gilbert families settled there in the late 1800s, and then the Case family built a Tudor-style home on the site, which speculator Captain Jack DeLysle later expanded in 1921. The house-turned-museum, restored to that era, now serves as a cultural and environmental learning center featuring the archeology and history of the island and Estero Bay. The Case family's inground swimming pool was excavated and is the site's centerpiece display, showing the layers of shells that trace the area's early cultural history. The Mound House staff offers various tours and ecology and history programs.

451 Connecticut St., Fort Myers Beach 33931
239-765-0865
moundhouse.org

TIP
Take the boat tour, leaving from Fish Tale Marina, 7225 Estero Blvd.,
Fort Myers Beach 33931, to Mound House and Mound Key,
thought to be the capital of the Calusa Indian nation.
Call 239-765-0865 for reservations.

SEE REMNANTS
OF AN EARLY RELIGIOUS COMMUNE

Following his service in the Union Army's medical corps during the Civil War, physician-turned-religious leader Dr. Cyrus Teed sought an isolated location for his sect. In 1894, Teed—who had changed his name to Koresh in 1869—established a utopian communal society in what is now Estero. Teed envisioned a thirty-four-square-mile settlement with ten million people, but he never managed to gather more than a couple hundred. One downfall was that the Koreshans believed in celibacy. Of the original fifty buildings, thirteen remain, including Teed's home, at the Koreshan State Park. Koreshans also believed that man lived on the interior of the world, facing the solar system within. At the historic site, visitors can see a hollow globe illustrating this theory. While there, take advantage of the park's nature trails, boat ramp, canoeing, fishing, camping, and special programs.

U.S. 41 S., Estero 33928
239-992-0311
floridastateparks.org/koreshan

TIP
The Koreshan Unity Settlement Historic District was named to the National Register of Historic Places in 1976. Take a paddling tour from the settlement to Mound Key, believed to have been the capital of the Calusa Indians. Mound Key is also listed on the National Register.

TAKE IN
A VILLAGE OF YESTERYEAR

Since 1984, the Sanibel Historical Village & Museum has been moving buildings from their original sites to the museum's campus. The cluster of structures, arranged as a village, tells the story of the island from the time of the Calusa Indians to the pioneer farming days of the 1800s and 1900s. The 1896 schoolhouse, the oldest building on display, later became a theater. Burnap Cottage, built in 1898, once held Sunday services. Other structures tell of everyday life and are furnished with period antiques. Open November through mid-August, the museum has varying hours, so call ahead. Historic museums of a more traditional nature are found in Cape Coral, Pine Island, Useppa Island, and Fort Myers.

Sanibel Historical Village
& Museum
950 Dunlop Rd., Sanibel 33957
239-472-4648
sanibelmuseum.org

Cape Coral Historical Museum
544 Cultural Park Blvd.,
Cape Coral 33990
239-772-7037
capecoralhistoricalmuseum.org

Museum of the Islands
5728 Sesame Dr., Bokeelia 33922
239-283-1525
museumoftheislands.com

Barbara Sumwalt Museum
Useppa Island/Bokeelia 33922
239-283-9600
useppahs.org

IMAG History & Science Center
2000 Cranford Ave., Fort Myers 33916
239-243-0043
i-sci.org

WALK IN
HISTORY'S FOOTSTEPS

"It's entertainment that's historically correct," says Gina Taylor, describing the True Tours she founded in 2010. A preservationist at heart, she wants to tell people the story beyond Thomas Edison's influence on the area. Her one-mile walking tours feature River District bygones, architecture, and pioneering women, plus, of course, there's the obligatory haunted history tour. For visitors who want to know more beyond downtown, the Flavors of Matlacha tour starts with seafood samples that are harvested from local waters and continues by informing how nature inspires this colorful artist colony adjacent to Pine Island. Call for dates, times, and starting locations of all tours and to make reservations.

True Tours at The Franklin Shops, 2200 First St., Fort Myers 33901
239-945-0405
truetours.net

TIP
For non-walkers, Arm Chair Tour guides make onsite visual presentations.

HEAR OF EARLY STRUGGLES
FOR EDUCATION

The Williams Academy Black History Museum occupies a two-room white wooden building that dates to 1942 and served as an addition to Southwest Florida's first African American government-funded school. After many years of disrepair, the building was moved to Roberto Clemente Park—a fitting location, since the Puerto Rican outfielder played baseball at nearby Terry Park and stayed in local homes when he wasn't allowed to stay at the team's segregated hotel. The school was restored in 2001 to become a museum to enlighten visitors of early struggles for education. The museum's timeline measures the achievements and acknowledges "firsts" in the community. Artifacts and photos tell the story from first settler Nelson Tillus to present-day sports heroes such as football star Deion Sanders, who grew up in Fort Myers.

1936 Henderson Ave., Fort Myers
239-332-8778
facebook.com/WilliamsAcademyBlackHistoryMuseum/

PHOTOGRAPH
HISTORIC LIGHTHOUSES

More than just navigation aids, lighthouses along the Gulf Coast serve as romantic reminders of the perils of the sea. The Sanibel Lighthouse and Keeper's Quarters (circa 1884) punctuates the eastern end of the island and was one of the first lighthouses north of Key West on the west coast of Florida. The original ironwork was headed to the island on a ship that sank about two miles off Sanibel. Most of it was recovered to build the ninety-eight-foot tower. Another light on the National Register of Historic Places, Port Boca Grande Lighthouse (circa 1890) sits forty-four feet tall on Gasparilla Island's southern tip in a cupola above a two-story keeper's dwelling, which now serves as a historical museum. Two miles north is the Boca Grande Rear Range Light (circa 1932). All three lights remain in service. Another, the Gasparilla Island Lighthouse (circa 1888), is being restored.

Sanibel Lighthouse Beach Park
110 Periwinkle Way, Sanibel 33957
239-472-3700
mysanibel.com

Port Boca Grande Lighthouse
Gasparilla State Park,
880 Belcher Rd., Boca Grande 33921
941-964-0060
barrierislandparkssociety.org

Gasparilla Island Lighthouse
220 Gulf Blvd., Boca Grande 33921
941-964-0060
barrierislandparkssociety.org

ADMIRE THE ARTIST
AND HIS CONTRIBUTIONS

A forerunner of the pop art movement, American painter, sculptor, and graphic artist Robert Rauschenberg lived and worked on Captiva Island from 1970 until his death in 2008. While he started with one-man shows in the '50s in New York, he eventually mounted exhibits around the world, including retrospectives in the Smithsonian American Art Museum, the Solomon R. Guggenheim Museum, and the Metropolitan Museum of Art. He received the prestigious National Medal of Arts (1993), the Leonardo da Vinci World Award of Arts (1995), the Praemium Imperiale (1998), and a Grammy for a Talking Heads album cover (1983). In 2004, the gallery at Florida SouthWestern State College was renamed the Bob Rauschenberg Gallery, celebrating a longtime friendship with the artist who, from the 1980s, often displayed his work in the gallery.

8099 College Pkwy., # L, Fort Myers 33919
239-489-9313
rauschenberggallery.com

TIP
The Fish House on Captiva Island, originally owned and used as a studio by political cartoonist J. N. "Ding" Darling and later by Rauschenberg, is now the site of the Rauschenberg Foundation Artist in Residency Program. For details, visit rauschenbergfoundation.org/residency.

GET TO KNOW THE COMMUNITY
THROUGH ITS PUBLIC ART

Public art helps define a community's culture. Perhaps it was started in Southwest Florida when *Rachel at the Well* was placed at the entrance to Edison Park. Many years later, *Uncommon Friends* became the centerpiece of Centennial Park. It pays tribute to three famous friends and Fort Myers winter residents: Henry Ford, Harvey Firestone, and Thomas Edison. One of Fort Myers's most intriguing sculptures, *Caloosahatchee Manuscript,* graces the entrance of the historic post office/federal courthouse building. The two metal cylinders with perforated letters cast shadows on nearby buildings when sunlight hits. At night, they are lighted so the shadows illuminate the front of the building. The Latin words on one cylinder are the names of plants Edison experimented with as possible sources of rubber. The second cylinder features Creek native language passages chronicling the Seminoles' migration in Florida.

TIP
For details on a self-guided public arts walking tour,
visit artswfl.com/public-art-2/fort-myers-river-district-public-art-2/walking-tour/walking-tour.

FIND NATURE
IN ART

Nature can greatly influence how we look at life. For area artists—whether writers, songwriters, fine artists, or craftspeople—it often emerges in the final product. Peruse local galleries to find the most authentic souvenirs of the area's natural surroundings. Captiva's Jungle Drums Gallery, for instance, holds a wildlife-themed collection of art fashioned from wood, metal, glass, and clay. In Matlacha, Wild Child Art Gallery features contemporary works produced by artists who take inspiration from their environment. The Tower Gallery on Sanibel Island showcases twenty-three artists inspired by nature to produce two- and three-dimensional works.

Jungle Drums Gallery
11532 Andy Rosse Ln.,
Captiva 33924
239-395-2266
jungledrumsgallery.com

Wild Child Art Gallery
4625 Pine Island Rd.,
Matlacha 33993
239-283-6006
wildchildartgallery.com

Tower Gallery
751 Tarpon Bay Rd., Sanibel 33957
239-472-4557
towergallery.net

TIP
The art of third-generation jeweler Scot Congress takes a different form. Shop his Sealife collection at Congress Jewelers, 2075 Periwinkle Way, Sanibel, 33957, 239-472-4177, congressjewelers.com.

DISCONNECT
FROM THE MAINLAND

Disconnect from the world for a picnic, fishing, and sunset on the Sanibel Causeway. Prior to the bridge's construction and opening in 1963, a ferry operated from Punta Rassa on the mainland. The building of the three-mile causeway at a cost of $2.73 million came with much consternation from island residents, who thought the connection to the mainland would ruin the beauty and isolation of the island. The causeway's drawbridge was replaced in 2007 by a seventy-foot-high span bridge, which became the tallest point in the county. The new causeway also replaced the original sections, which were dropped offshore to create artificial reefs in San Carlos Bay and the Gulf of Mexico.

18700 McGregor Blvd., Fort Myers 33908
239-533-8655
leegov.com/dot/tolls/lw_facilities/san

FUN FACT
Today, Sanibel still has no traffic signals,
street lights or high rise buildings.

WONDER
AT NORTH AMERICA'S
ONLY SEASHELL MUSEUM

Dr. R. Tucker Abbott, former assistant curator of the Department of Mollusks at the Smithsonian Institution, died two weeks before the 1995 grand opening of the Bailey-Matthews National Shell Museum on Sanibel. As its founding director, he brought the quality and professionalism to the museum that is his legacy. Bailey-Matthews is the only museum in North America dedicated solely to seashells. It contains the largest collection of shells on the continent and tells the story of mollusks throughout the world. Scientists and amateurs alike can study seashells in the fine exhibits, while children explore the hands-on learning lab. The museum's first honorary fundraising chairman, the late actor and conchologist Raymond Burr, donated a few cowries and cones from his island home in Fiji. Following his death, NBC *TODAY* show weatherman and TV personality Willard Scott took on his role.

3075 Sanibel-Captiva Rd., Sanibel 33957
239-395-2233
shellmuseum.org

TIP
The museum offers beach walks and lectures.

EXPERIENCE SCIENCE AND HISTORY
TOGETHER

Southwest Florida likes to recycle everything, and that goes for cans, bottles, plastic, cardboard, newspapers, boats, bridges—even buildings. A 1950s water plant became the Imaginarium Science Center in 1995. Recently, it transitioned to the IMAG History & Science Center. The science part is a hands-on experience with marine life, a weather forecasting studio, a dinosaur dig, an animal lab, Mini Museum for young children, and even an aquarium installed by the crew from TV's Animal Planet show *Tanked*. It features a replica of the USS *Mohawk*, a WWII warship sunk off Sanibel Island to create an artificial reef. Kids of all ages explore the various stations, see live animal encounters, and watch 3D movies. The Southwest Florida Museum of History meshed with the site in the transition, adding popular exhibits that examine the early Calusa and Seminoles, as well as WWII exhibits. A new exhibit will feature a virtual reality walk through 1856 Fort Myers.

2000 Cranford Ave., Fort Myers 33916
239-321-7420
i-sci.org

GAZE AT GRAND ARCHITECTURE
WHILE ATTENDING AN EVENT

When you see a building of Neoclassical Revival architecture with massive columns in south Florida, you know there has to be an interesting history to match the grandeur. The site upon which the Sidney & Berne Davis Art Center stands in the downtown River District was originally a Native American Calusa settlement. It later housed soldiers in Fort Myers during the Civil War. In 1933, it became a United States Post Office and later a federal courthouse. When the government built a new courthouse, the abandoned building fell into disrepair. In 2003 a project to bring back the old splendor created a modern arts facility. The center hosts art exhibits, lecture series, a film festival, a fashion show, education festivals, concerts, and other special events year-round.

2301 First St., Fort Myers 33901
239-333-1933
sbdac.com

TIP
When touring the building, head upstairs to see handprints from its 1933 construction. No one knows why, but each hand has six fingers.

TOUR THE GRANDE DAME
OF BOCA GRANDE

Topping the list of *Travel + Leisure* magazine's Best Resort Hotels in Florida, The Gasparilla Inn & Club reigns as the grande dame of Boca Grande. Since 1913, the inn has welcomed guests to Gasparilla Island. Visitors step back in time as they walk past the neoclassical pillars of the pale yellow, wooden-framed building with its gabled roof entrance and witness for the first time the lobby of rich dark wood and native pecky cypress in the bar. Ah, Old Florida coastal elegance. Named to the National Register of Historic Places as the oldest wooden hotel in Florida, the inn comprises sixty-three rooms, sixteen cottages, and six Sharp Houses, named for the Sharp family, descendants of the Du Ponts, who regularly wintered on Boca Grande. Other famous and longstanding guests include Katharine Hepburn, Thomas Edison, Henry Ford, J. P. Morgan, and the presidential Bush family.

500 Palm Ave., Boca Grande 33921
941-964-4500
the-gasparilla-inn.com

TIP
The Gasparilla Inn & Club takes its name from the legendary eighteenth-century Spanish pirate José Gaspar, who reputedly plundered the seas and stashed his treasure on Gasparilla Island. The inn offers history tours to the public on Tuesdays and Fridays.

SLEEP WHERE THE FAMOUS
HAVE REJUVENATED

'Tween Waters Inn Island Resort & Spa has renovated six cottages with select décor to honor famous former guests and visitors: aviator Charles Lindbergh and his wife, author Anne Morrow Lindbergh; President Teddy Roosevelt; ornithologist Roger Tory Peterson; and Pulitzer Prize-winning cartoonist and conservationist J. N. "Ding" Darling. The Lindbergh-themed cottage draws from his aviation career and features a bomber leather sofa, while Anne's influence materializes in an airy seaside motif reminiscent of the time she spent researching her famous book *Gift from the Sea.* Roosevelt came to Captiva to fish the world-renowned back bay waters, which are now named Roosevelt Channel. His cottage appeals to the passions of anglers and outdoor enthusiasts, featuring log furniture. The décor had to revolve around birds for ornithologist and naturalist Peterson, the author of *A Field Guide to the Birds.* Darling's cottage and adjacent studio depict his love of nature and showcase scanned prints of his original drawings.

15951 Captiva Dr., Captiva 33924
239-472-5161
tween-waters.com

TIP
On the National Register of Historic Places,
the cottages are quite popular, so reserve early.

READ BETWEEN
THE SHELVES

Libraries can be treasure troves of history and culture, and that holds especially true at a couple of Southwest Florida libraries. Captiva Memorial Library holds a replica of the *Santiva* mail boat. It delivered mail and provisions to the islands from 1936 until 1963, when the Sanibel Causeway opened. The exhibit features a short film about daily twentieth-century life. Multiple touch screens cover the island's history, including farming and fishing in the 1900s. Going back quite a bit further in history, displays at the Johann Fust Community Library in Boca Grande contain a page from *The Book of the Dead* (first century B.C.), a clay tablet with cuneiform script, a leaf from the Gutenberg Bible (1454), and two framed pages from *The Ship of Fools* (1570).

Captiva Memorial Library
11560 Chapin Ln., Captiva 33924
239-533-4890
leegov.com/library/branches/cv

Johann Fust Community Library
1040 West 10th St.,
Boca Grande 33921
941-964-2488
jfcl.org

TIP
Next door to the Captiva library, peek inside the windows of the 1903 Captiva Chapel by the Sea, which is open from November to April. It first served as a school and then as a church when the circuit preacher came around. Adjacent to the chapel is the Historic Captiva Cemetery. It holds the graves of the early Captiva pioneers.

LISTEN TO THE BEAT
OF A BYGONE ERA

Local historians are upbeat about the restoration of McCollum Hall (circa 1938), once a center of the Dunbar community east of downtown Fort Myers. Built by Clifford McCollum Sr., it was part of the Chitlin' Circuit, a name given to segregated venues where famous African Americans once performed. From the '30s through the '50s, the second-floor dance hall vibrated to the music of Duke Ellington, Louis Armstrong, B. B. King, Count Basie, and other entertainers who performed there. It was the "in" scene for black WWII soldiers. In the '80s, the hall was subdivided into rooms for boarders. It has also been used for high school proms and rehearsals for Dunbar High School bands. This historic landmark has received a Florida Division of Historic Preservation grant and is undergoing revitalization to become a center for retail businesses and services.

2701 Dr. Martin Luther King Jr. Blvd., Fort Myers 33916
cityftmyers.com/mccollum

RETROGRADE IN TIME
AT ROADSIDE ATTRACTIONS

Harold and Mildred Crant began selling seashells and crafts at the Shell Factory in Bonita Springs in 1938. Through hurricanes, floods, fires, and foreclosure/bankruptcy, The Shell Factory & Nature Park, now located on seventeen acres in North Fort Myers, has evolved from an Old Florida roadside attraction to a shopping/entertainment center under current owners Tom and Pam Cronin. More than 700,000 annual visitors enjoy an eclectic museum, modern amusements such as zip lining, shops and restaurants, and a nature park. Another popular roadside attraction, Everglades Wonder Gardens, preserves its legacy while looking forward. Opened by Bill and Les Piper in 1936, the roadside zoo ran for three generations under the Piper family until it became a nonprofit in 2015. Gone are most of the animals, including the fourteen-foot "Big Joe," but thirty-seven of his alligator friends remain with a flock of flamingoes, plus reptiles, other birds, and a lush garden.

The Shell Factory & Nature Park
2787 N. Tamiami Trl.,
North Fort Myers 33903
239-995-2141
shellfactory.com

Everglades Wonder Gardens
27180 Old 41 Rd.,
Bonita Springs 34135
239-992-2591
evergladeswondergardens.com

TIP
Dogs are allowed everywhere at The Shell Factory except in the nature park.

Photo Credit:
Courtesy of Lee County Visitor &
Convention Bureau

SHOPPING AND FASHION

SCOOP UP NEPTUNE'S TREASURES
AT SHELL SHOPS

If you didn't find that perfect seashell, sand dollar, or starfish while beachcombing along the area's fifty miles of white sand beaches, hit the shell shops to scoop up some of Neptune's treasures. The Shell Factory & Nature Park, which opened as an Old Florida roadside attraction in 1938, offers all things made with shells from the seven seas. Specimen shells, jewelry, home goods, and shell crafts can be found here if you're in North Fort Myers. On Sanibel, the Joffe family opened She Sells Sea Shells in 1976—one of the first of many to follow on the island. Shoppers can find shells and exotic sea life, jewelry, books, craft supplies, clothing, handbags, and an extensive collection of handmade shell crafts and ornaments.

Shell Factory & Nature Park
2787 N. Tamiami Trl.,
North Fort Myers 33903
239-995-2141
shellfactory.com

She Sells Sea Shells
1157 Periwinkle Way,
Sanibel 33957
239-472-6991
sanibelshellcrafts.com

TIP
Shell crafts can be purchased from the Sanibel Shell Crafters, who meet Mondays at the Sanibel Community House, 2173 Periwinkle Way, Sanibel 33957, 239-472-2155.

SCRUTINIZE THE PERFECT TRAVEL OUTFIT
AT SANIBEL WOMEN'S BOUTIQUE

Probably the most successful business to grow out of Southwest Florida, Chico's FAS, Inc., caters to fashion-savvy women. Known for its comfortable, stylish clothing that travels well, the franchise started in 1983 on Sanibel Island. Husband and wife team Marvin and Helene Gralnick opened a tiny gift shop at Periwinkle Place featuring Mexican folk art and sweaters. The sweaters sold like crazy, but the artwork—not so much. Two years later they opened a women's clothing store on Captiva, followed by franchising. Now more than 1,500 locations are spread throughout the United States and Canada. The firm also owns White House Black Market and Soma. While the corporate headquarters is located in Fort Myers, you can still visit the original shop on Sanibel or one of the multiple locations in the Fort Myers area.

Periwinkle Place, 2075 Periwinkle Way, Ste. 4, Sanibel 33957
239-472-0202
chicos.com

TIP
To find Chico's best bargains, visit the store at Miromar Outlets, 10801 Corkscrew Rd., Estero 33928, 239-949-2252.

HELP OTHERS
SUPPORT THEMSELVES

Purchases that help alleviate poverty and marginalization make shopping just that much more rewarding. He, She & Me carries handcrafted goods using sustainable materials made by women who live in third-world nations. This shop imports these handcrafted items to help these artists, their families, and developing countries around the world. Artisans from up to thirty different countries create products, each with a unique story to tell. Purchasing fair trade items contributes to eradicating poverty, eliminating human trafficking, educating children, and supporting marginalized people, according to owner Melody Hull. Artisans turn bamboo, metal, bicycle chains, magazines, cloth, wood, and stone into accessories, clothing, home décor, and jewelry.

2070 Bayside Pkwy., Fort Myers 33901
239-332-3887
hesheandme.com

DECORATE
YOUR NEST

After managing the Broadway Palm Dinner Theatre for many years, Susan Johnson decided to stage her own production. In 2011, she and her mother, artist Jean Bynes Porpora, opened The Nest Home and Garden. While Porpora has since passed away, her family remains passionate about the artwork and décor they offer for homes and gardens. Artsy and fun accessories fill the store nestled near The Franklin Shops on First Street in the downtown River District. The most popular items include wall plaques and pillows, but don't forget to pick up candles and soaps to decorate your nest.

2214 First St., Fort Myers 33901
239-226-1314
thenesthomeandgarden.com

UNCOVER
A NEW OLD TREASURE

Inquisitiveness brings shoppers into The Curiosity Shop to uncover fashion history and treasures from the past. This boutique buys and sells vintage clothing, jewelry, and accessories from the 1800s to the 1970s. Don't be daunted by the jam-packed shop—it just means there are more treasures to find in the many cases and racks of clothing. Darien and James Workman will provide the expertise to assist in locating the perfect item for an upcoming party or special occasion. Most buyers are looking for fashions from the 1920s, Victorian era, and 1950s, says James. No matter what you seek, the shop offers a peek into the past that's lots more fun than going to a museum. Do take time to marvel at the intricate and detailed 1859 black corseted mourning dress.

1939 Suwannee Ave., Fort Myers 33901
239-672-0271
facebook.com/thecuriosityshopdarien

TAKE HOME
THE SCENT AND TASTE OF FLORIDA

For a potent taste of Fort Myers to take or send home, visit family-owned Sun Harvest Citrus. It packs and ships citrus items to friends and family throughout the United States and Canada, but the realm of products goes far beyond fresh fruit. Upon entering the packinghouse, the sweet smell of citrus revs up your senses. Sample freshly squeezed juices, tasty orange or lime soft-serve cones, and fruit smoothies. Other tempting gourmet treats include hot sauces, jams, jellies, marmalades, honey, candies, and even Florida wines made from tropical fruit. In the non-edible department, find souvenirs such as wind chimes, handbags, totes, Florida books, plush animals, body care products, soaps, and coastal home décor. Love the mermaid trend? Inventory is always changing to meet what's hot.

14810 Metro Pkwy., Fort Myers 33912
239-768-2686
sunharvestcitrus.com

TIP
The most popular non-edible item is the Sun Harvest Citrus lip balm. Best time for bargains is in the summer.

GATHER FRESH HARVEST
AT LOCAL FARMERS MARKETS

Local farmers markets offer the freshest tastes you can find in Southwest Florida without picking your own. Each Thursday morning the vegetables, fruits, flowers, seafood, and an array of other local goods make for a colorful, sweetly scented scene at the downtown Fort Myers Farmers Market under the U.S. 41 Caloosahatchee Bridge at Centennial Park. The oldest farmers market in the area, it was started in 1994 by the Fort Myers Community Downtown Redevelopment Agency. The year-round market closes only on Thanksgiving Day. A number of other popular markets in the area run in season, typically October through May. Check their websites for days and hours of operation.

Centennial Park, Heitman and First Sts., Fort Myers 33901
239-321-7100
buylocallee.com

Bonita Springs Farmers Market
Saturdays at Promenade
26851 S. Bay Dr., Bonita Springs 34134
buylocallee.com

Cape Coral Farmers Market
Saturdays at Dixie Roadhouse
SE 47th Ter. & SE 10th Pl., Cape Coral 33904
239-549-6900
capecoralfarmersmarket.com

Coconut Point Farmers Market
Thursdays at 23106 Fashion Dr., Estero 33928
buylocallee.com

Fenway South Farmers Market
Wednesdays, JetBlue Park
11500 Fenway South Dr., Fort Myers 33913
buylocallee.com

GreenMarket
Saturdays at Alliance for the Arts
10091 McGregor Blvd., Fort Myers 33919
239-939-2787
artinlee.org/visit/greenmarket

Koreshan State Park Farmers Market
Sundays
3800 Corkscrew Rd., Estero 33928
floridastateparks.org

Lakes Regional Park
Fridays
7330 Gladiolus Dr., Fort Myers 33908
buylocallee.com

Rodes Farmers Market
Saturdays & Sundays
3756 Bonita Beach Rd., Bonita Springs 34134
41markets.com

Surfside Sunset Market
Tuesday nights, 2–7 p.m.
Veteran's Pkwy. & Surfside Blvd.,
Cape Coral 33991
capecoralfarmersmarket.com

PICK UP GOLF ESSENTIALS
TO START YOUR ROUND OUT RIGHT

If the 150-plus golf courses in Southwest Florida are any indication, golf is HUGE here. And where there are golf courses, there must be an array of shops to purchase equipment, shoes, and other apparel. The Golf Guys offer brands from Adidas to Zero, including Bridgestone, Cleveland Golf, ECCO, Golf Buddy, New Balance, Nike, Puma, Skechers, and Wilson Golf. Open daily except major holidays, this locally owned shop also takes walk-in customers for club fittings and fixes, including shaft repairs while you wait. The staff can fit all major companies' clubs, including the higher-end PXG irons and woods. The Golf Guys have a large inventory of new and used golf gear, plus a putting green and two hitting bays that allow staff to best serve their customers.

3440 Renaissance Blvd., Bonita Springs 34134
239-948-9840
golfbonitaspringsfl.com

COLOR YOUR WORLD
WITH A BIT OF LEOMA

For a potent, one-stop taste of quirky little Matlacha, visit Leoma Lovegrove Gallery & Gardens. Take an eco-tour of the area's aquatic preserve, cast a fishing line into Matlacha Pass, paint a coconut postcard to send home, sample some coconut ice cream, and, oh yes, peruse the gallery. Leoma Lovegrove is as colorful as her fine art paintings. If you need inspiration, a stroll through the gardens will enlighten and brighten your day with Leoma's effervescence and splashes of color—everywhere! A tropical impressionist/expressionist, she paints oversized fish, birds, sea life, scenes of Florida, and portraits. Her favorites are The Beatles. Other portraits include one of President Jimmy Carter, which hangs in his presidential library, and that of Sir Richard Branson, which is displayed in the Virgin Airlines headquarters in London.

Matlacha Pass Aquatic Preserve, 4637 Pine Island Rd., Matlacha 33993
239-938-5655
leomalovegrove.com

TIP
Impressed with Leoma's colorful style, Bealls Department Store developed a full line of products from clothing to home goods to showcase her artwork. To participate in one of the gallery's frequent events, check the website.

GET TRAPPED
IN RETAIL THERAPY HEAVEN

Only the name is the same at the 1937 Franklin Hardware Store. Today's Franklin Shops in the downtown River District is a retail emporium presenting two floors of edgy, sweet, and casual items—a pleasant juxtaposition of historic and new. Merchandise categories include Body & Soul, Fine Art & Glass, Jewelry & Accessories, Books & Music, Gifts & Novelties, Stationery & Cards, Fashion & Style, and Home & Patio. Some of the more unusual items in the shops are sculptures of masking tape and wire and works made from reclaimed objects described as "happy and also charmingly disturbing," says Cornelia Reinhardt of The Franklin Shops. Funky, cool, and entertaining, the emporium's creative vibe appeals to hipsters, connoisseurs, and treasure-hunters.

2200 First St., Fort Myers 33901
239-333-3130
thefranklinshops.com

TIP
The shops host live art and music performances during Art Walk (first Friday evening of the month) and Music Walk (third Friday evening of the month). For the many other events, check the website.

CATCH MAJOR LEAGUE BASEBALL NOVELTIES
IN TEAM SPORTS SHOPS

Each year during spring training, sports fans can stock up on Major League Baseball memorabilia at the Red Sox and Twins team stores. While hats and T-shirts are the most popular items, pennants, magnets, pins, and baseballs with logos printed on them fill the shelves and racks. Many articles are designed specifically for spring training in Florida and can't be found at their northern home parks. Be sure to get an item before the game starts, since players are happy to autograph them during their warm-ups and practices.

Boston Red Sox Team Store
Jet Blue Park, 11581 Daniels Pkwy.,
Fort Myers 33913
239-226-4732
boston.redsox.mlb.com/bos/ballpark/
jetblue_park.jsp

Minnesota Twins Team Store
Hammond Stadium, 14400 Ben C
Pratt / 6 Mile Cypress Pkwy.,
Fort Myers 33912
239-768-4210
minnesota.twins.mlb.com/spring_
training/ballpark.jsp?c_id=min

TIP
On the last day of spring training, the teams offer a 50 percent discount on all items. Some discounts go deeper just before the teams load up their trucks to return north for the regular season.

SELECT THE TACKLE
TO REEL IN THE FISH

There are big fish and little fish in the sea of Southwest Florida fishing gear retail. The big fish is Bass Pro Shops, a destination unto itself. From lures to boats, the shop offers the full gamut of gear for the avid outdoors person. The Fort Myers store features a twelve-thousand-gallon saltwater aquarium, a nineteen-thousand-gallon freshwater aquarium, an indoor three-lane archery range, plus the Islamorada Fish Company Restaurant. Bass Pro may have the largest selection, but smaller shops often have the best local knowledge. Lehr's Economy Tackle, for instance, offers name-brand gear, rod and reel repair, and know-how that dates back to the store's opening in 1957. Anderson's Bait and Tackle features gear repair and bait, including baby blue crabs to catch tarpon. Norm Zeigler's Fly Shop provides all the products, services, and expertise for fly fishing.

Bass Pro Shops
10040 Gulf Center Dr.,
Fort Myers 33913
239-461-7800
basspro.com

Anderson's Bait and Tackle
15675 McGregor Blvd.,
Fort Myers 33908
239-334-3474
facebook.com/andersons.tackle

Lehr's Economy Tackle
1366 N. Tamiami Trl.,
North Fort Myers 33903
239-995-2280
lehrseconomytackle.com

Norm Zeigler's Fly Shop
2242 Periwinkle Way, Unit No. 1,
Sanibel 33957
239-472-6868
normzeiglersflyshop.com

EXPLORE THE MAZE OF BOOTHS
AT FLEA MARKETS

To find hidden booty that won't cost you a chest full of doubloons, shop at one of the local flea markets. Fleamasters Fleamarket holds nine hundred booths in more than 400,000 square feet of outdoor space. Featured items range from fresh fruits and vegetables to antiques. Treasure hunters uncover arts and crafts, home goods, clothing, jewelry, and collectibles, while outdoor enthusiasts find fishing and golf merchandise. Take respite and nourishment at one of twenty food booths and enjoy the entertainment at the recently added stage. Nearby in Bonita Springs, Flamingo Island Flea Market offers everything from clothing to home accessories in six hundred spaces. Six restaurants feature fresh produce and seafood. Both markets are open year-round Friday through Sunday.

Fleamasters Fleamarket
4135 Dr. Martin Luther King Jr.
Blvd., Fort Myers 33916
239-334-7001
fleamall.com

Flamingo Island Flea Market
11902 Bonita Beach Rd. SE,
Bonita Springs 34135
239-948-7799
flamingoisland.com

TIP
Festivals at the flea markets serve up food, music, and fun. Be sure to check the websites for upcoming events.

VIEW AND SUPPORT
LOCAL ARTS

For the most authentic souvenirs of your Fort Myers visit, shop local art cooperatives for one-of-a-kind objets d'art. At DAAS Co-op Art Gallery & Gifts, twenty-five artists plus one monthly local guest display in the 2,400-square-foot gallery. The locally produced art runs the full array of media—pottery, jewelry, sculpture, photography, abstract painting, and glass. Featured events include a monthly artist opening reception, a wine tasting, and a wine and art painting party. Next door, the Lee County Alliance for the Arts exists to grow the arts locally. It hosts month-long changing exhibitions. The gift shop sells fun and quirky items such as change purses and pocketbooks made from coffee filters and small landscapes created from objects found in Florida such as glass, bark, and pebbles.

DAAS Co-op
1400 Colonial Blvd., #84,
Fort Myers 33907
239-590-8645
daascoop.com

Lee County Alliance for the Arts
10091 McGregor Blvd.,
Fort Myers 33919
239-939-2787
artinlee.org

TIP
The Alliance for the Arts hosts a GreenMarket every Saturday year-round featuring locally grown, caught, and cultivated foods and other products. Check the website for dates and times.

PURCHASE ART
TO ASSIST PEOPLE IN CRISIS

Internationally renowned artists Romero Britto, Darryl Pottorf, and Robert Rauschenberg, the latter two of whom have lived on Captiva, have all donated works to the Arts for ACT Gallery and Boutique. Abuse Counseling and Treatment, Inc. (ACT), a nonprofit agency that provides shelter and support services for victims of domestic violence and sexual assault, owns and operates the gallery. It showcases some seventy-five local artists; proceeds go to help people in crisis. The gallery features contemporary, original art including pop art, surrealism, naïve and primitive art, and abstract expressionism in an array of mediums, plus a limited amount of three-dimensional art such as gourd art, raku, and clay. Wander through the shop to find silver and glass bead jewelry, handmade fine crafts, art clothing, handbags, and shoes.

2265 First St., Fort Myers 33901
239-337-5050
artsforactgallery.com

TIP
A highlight each year is the Arts for ACT Fine Art Auction, which features celebrity auctioneers. Past hosts have included Sharon Stone, Meryl Streep, and Lily Tomlin. Check the gallery's website for the event date.

CHOOSE COMFORTABLE CLOTHING
FOR SUBTROPICAL CLIMES

The three "Cs" of Florida resort beachwear are casual, comfortable, and colorful. Keep in mind Fort Myers has a subtropical climate with year-round temperatures averaging 77.5° F—66° F in the winter and 87° F in the summer. Find attire to fit the occasion and weather at the Florida-based department store Bealls (pronounced "Bells"). Among the brands featured are colorful fashions from Coral Bay, Julian Taylor, Jamaican marine wildlife artist Guy Harvey, and local impressionist artist Leoma Lovegrove. Other options can be found on Fort Myers Beach at Local Color, which carries clothing, jewelry, and accessories for the beach. Fresh Produce stores stock easy-to-wear women's clothing and accessories for the resort, beach, or a day on the water. Everything But Water features various brands of swimwear as well as lacy cover-ups, floral print sundresses, and vibrant pareos.

TIP
To look your best in this climate, remember to wear a hat, sunglasses, and sunscreen and to keep hydrated.

Bealls Department Stores
70-plus locations throughout Florida
800-569-9038
beallsflorida.com

Local Color
1021 Estero Blvd., Unit B, Fort Myers Beach 33931
239-463-9199
facebook.com/localcolorfmb

Fresh Produce
Periwinkle Place, 2075 Periwinkle Way,
Sanibel 33957
239-395-1839
freshproduceclothes.com

Everything But Water
Aqua Beachwear, 2075 Periwinkle Way, #12,
Sanibel 33957
239-472-2676
everythingbutwater.com

FIND GREAT SAVINGS
IN A LIVELY SETTING

Miromar Outlets is a destination shopping center that receives visitors from around the world. The Mediterranean architecture with open-air walkways in a subtropical setting showcases discounted upscale shops and hosts a wide range of events. Miromar houses more than 140 top designer and brand-name stores: Bloomingdale's, Chico's, Calvin Klein, Michael Kors, Neiman Marcus, Ralph Lauren, and Saks Fifth Avenue, to name a few. Restaurants offer a variety of indoor and outdoor settings for Mexican, Italian, Japanese, and American cuisine. Recurring events for fitness, concerts, and holidays happen year-round. Shoppers can even catch a water skiing show.

10801 Corkscrew Rd., Estero 33928
239-948-3766
miromaroutlets.com

TIP
Pick up a VIP Savings pamphlet offering additional savings at the management office.

SHOP FOR THE EXTRAORDINARY
AND BOLSTER NONPROFIT GIFT SHOPS

The best souvenirs can often be found in the nonprofit gift shops. The Bailey-Matthews National Shell Museum, for instance, stocks jewelry, books, stationery, and home décor—all with a seashell motif, of course. The Edison & Ford Winter Estates has two stores and a garden shop offering a variety of items relating to history, science, literature, gardening, and children. The garden shop carries plants propagated from Edison's botanical garden, which featured plants that friends originally sent him from around the world. At the IMAG History & Science Center, gifts reflect the visitor experience—from dinosaurs to marine life. At the J.N. "Ding" Darling National Wildlife Refuge nature store, clothing, books, jewelry, ornaments, and housewares showcase local fauna and flora.

Bailey-Matthews
National Shell Museum
3075 Sanibel-Captiva Rd.,
Sanibel 33957
239-395-2233
shellmuseum.org

Edison & Ford Winter Estates
2350 McGregor Blvd.,
Fort Myers 33901
239-334-7419
edisonfordwinterestates.org

IMAG History & Science Center
2000 Cranford Ave.,
Fort Myers 33916
239-243-0043
i-sci.org

J.N. "Ding" Darling
National Wildlife Refuge
Educational Center, 1 Wildlife Dr.,
Sanibel 33957
239-472-1100
dingdarlingsociety.org

SUGGESTED
ITINERARIES

BEACH

To disconnect, throw down your towel at Bowman's Beach, 58

For action, get wet with Holiday Water Sports, 85

Go beachcombing for seashells at secluded Cayo Costa State Park, 63

Watch for wildlife at Lovers Key State Park, 61

Kick off your flip-flops and enjoy a cool one at the Tiki Bar, 23

NATURE

Go birding at Audubon's Corkscrew Swamp Sanctuary, 56

Seek serenity at J.N. "Ding" Darling National Wildlife Refuge, 61

Paddle like the natives once did on the Great Calusa Blueway, 75

Island hop to watch wildlife with Captiva Cruises, 79

Take a journey with Adventures in Paradise, 69

Experience the area with a Pure Florida master naturalist, 69

Hit the trail with the Sanibel-Captiva Conservation Foundation, 60

Watch a natural miracle with Turtle Time, 83

HISTORY

Be amazed and inspired at the Edison & Ford Winter Estates, 88

Peel back the layers of history at Mound House, 92

Learn about the religious sect that inhabited the Koreshan State Park, 93

Walk in native footsteps along the Calusa Heritage Trail, 91

Hear the tales of early Fort Myers settlers living at the Burroughs Home, 89

Sleuth out history as you walk the town with True Tours, 95

CULTURE

WATER ACTIVITIES

FAMILY FUN

SPORTS

CUISINE

ACTIVITIES
BY SEASON

SPRING

Kayak the calm waters of the Great Calusa Blueway, 75

Splash in the waters with your furry friend at Dog Beach, 58

Stroll along the boardwalk at Audubon Corkscrew Swamp Sanctuary, 56

Be astonished at the Sanibel Shell Fair, 46

Walk the links at Fort Myers Golf Course, 78

Take a nature walk at Lovers Key State Park, 61

Catch the fun at spring training baseball, 72

SUMMER

Bite into MangoMania, 47

Identify your seashells at the Bailey-Mathews National Shell Museum, 102

Have an adventure at Babcock Wilderness, 69

Fish for tarpon (April to July), 124

Boat the Intracoastal Waterway, 75

Be amazed by the inventions at the Edison & Ford Winter Estates, 88

Lace up for ice skating, 50

Tube it at Sun Splash Waterpark, 47

FALL

Get an eyeful at Art Walk, 36

Arrrrrrgh you ready for fun at the Pirate Festival?, 45

Bounce to the beat of Music Walk, 36

Bike along the miles of path on Sanibel Island, 60

Marvel at nature during "Ding" Darling Days, 47

Walk the historic side, 62

Fish for small or big game, 124

Carve a memory at the Fort Myers Beach Sand Sculpting Championship, 47

WINTER

Witness an endangered West Indian Manatee, 80

Line the parade route during the Edison Festival of Light, 46

Bless the fleet during the Fort Myers Beach Shrimp Festival, 2

Become an artist during ArtFest, 47

Secure an autograph during spring training baseball, 72

Camp while the weather's great, 62

Check off a rare bird from your list, 64

Adore the cuteness at the Burrowing Owl Festival, 47

While Southwest Florida has marvelous year-round weather for outdoor activities, the summer and fall months occur in the rainy season, when activities go according to Mother Nature's schedule.

INDEX